NEW HAVEN FREE PUBLIC LIBRARY

3 000 09583 5087

35000095835087

D1605173

DUE

OFFICIALLY WITHDRAWN
NEW HAVEN FREE PUBLIC LIBRARY

FAIR HAVEN LIBRARY
182 GRAND AVENUE
NEW HAVEN CT 06513

Marshall Cavendish

Copyright © 2011 Marshall Cavendish Corporation

Published by Marshall Cavendish Reference
An imprint of Marshall Cavendish Corporation

All rights reserved.

No part of this publication may be reproduced, stored in a retrieval system or transmitted, in any form or by any means, electronic, mechanical, photocopying, recording, or otherwise, without the prior permission of the copyright owner. Request for permission should be addressed to the Publisher, Marshall Cavendish Corporation, 99 White Plains Road, Tarrytown, NY 10591. Tel: (914) 332-8888, fax: (914) 332-1888.

Website: www.marshallcavendish.us

Library of Congress Cataloging-in-Publication Data
Ancient Rome : an illustrated history.
    p. cm.
  Includes index.
  ISBN 978-0-7614-7933-8 (alk. paper)
  1. Rome--History. 2. Rome--Civilization. 3. Rome--Social life and customs.
  DG78.A626 2010
  937--dc22

                 2010002925

Printed in Malaysia

14 13 12 11 10   1 2 3 4 5

MARSHALL CAVENDISH
Publisher: Paul Bernabeo
Project Editor: Brian Kinsey
Production Manager: Mike Esposito

THE BROWN REFERENCE GROUP PLC
Managing Editor: Tim Harris
Designer: Lynne Lennon
Picture Researcher: Laila Torsun
Indexer: Ann Barrett
Design Manager: David Poole
Editorial Director: Lindsey Lowe

This publication represents the opinions and views of the authors based on personal experience, knowledge, and research. The information in this book serves as a general guide only. The author and publisher have used their best efforts in preparing this book and disclaim liability rising directly and indirectly from the use and application of this book.

Other Marshall Cavendish Offices:

Marshall Cavendish International (Asia) Private Limited, 1 New Industrial Road, Singapore 536196 • Marshall Cavendish International (Thailand) Co Ltd. 253 Asoke, 12th Flr, Sukhumvit 21 Road, Klongtoey Nua, Wattana, Bangkok 10110, Thailand • Marshall Cavendish (Malaysia) Sdn Bhd, Times Subang, Lot 46, Subang Hi-Tech Industrial Park, Batu Tiga, 40000 Shah Alam, Selangor Darul Ehsan, Malaysia

Marshall Cavendish is a trademark of Times Publishing Limited

All websites were available and accurate when this book was sent to press.

PHOTOGRAPHIC CREDITS
Front Cover: iStockphoto: Studio Campo (background); **Shutterstock:** Ariy (main). **Back Cover: iStockphoto:** Studio Campo (background); **Shutterstock:** Ariy (main). **Inside: AKG:** 12, 14, 20, 50, 54, 57, 76, 79, 91, 96, 106, 109, 114, 119, Herve Champollion 35, 75, Keith Collie 92, Peter Connolly 63, 120, Gerard Degeorge 55, Jean-Paul Dumontier 103, Electa 46, 99, Tristan Lafrancis 23, Erich Lessing 9, 28, 38, 39, 69, 94, 101, 107, 112, 115, Museum Kalkriese 74, Nimtallah 88, 108, 113, Pirozzi 10, 81, 83, 110, Rabatti-Domingie 27t, 66, Jurgen Sorge 60; **Corbis:** 11, 33, Alantide Phototravel 41, Jonathan Blair 129, Burstein Collection 58, Gianni Dagli Orti 36, Araldo De Luca 48, 52, 67, Chris Hellier 43, Johansen Karuse/Archivo Iconographic, SA 40, Vanni Archive 53, Sandro Vannini 65, Roger Wood 45; **Mary Evans Picture Library:** 22t, 29, 47, 61, 71, 89; **Shutterstock:** Ariy 3, Konstantin Baskakpv 131, Ant Clausen 162, Lou Lou Photos 132, Olga Skalkina 34, Valeria73 1, Dmitry Zamorin 5; **Topham:** 18, 82, 90, AA World Travel Library 16, 98, 111, 127, Alinari 7, 15, 19, 31, 78, 87, 93, 104, ARPL 69, British Library/HIP 13, 25, 27b, 86, Museum of London 117, Michael Rhodes 80, Roger-Viollet 22b, 37, 51, 62, 105, 121, 125, 130, World History Archive 85; **Werner Forman:** 17, 122, 124, 133, British Museum 73, 95, Museo Nazionale Romano 77, 118, 123.

CONTENTS

937 ANCIENT
Ancient Rome :an illustrated
history.
35000095835087
FAIR HAVEN LIBRARY

FOREWORD

To begin a study of Roman history is to begin the study of Western civilization, and this introductory work provides a fine place to start. In truth, all roads lead not only to Rome, but from Rome. Upon Rome's extensive system of roads moved not just the building blocks of society and commerce, but also an invisible cargo of ideas that connected Roman society and later the Christian Church, early modern Europe, and all that followed.

Roman culture was syncretic from the beginning. The early years of monarchy (753–510 BCE) witnessed the amalgamation of Etruscans, Oscans, Sabines, and other Italic peoples. Bit by bit the Romans of the republican period (510 BCE–27 BCE) extended their imperium. By 270 BCE, Rome controlled the entire Italian Peninsula. The expansions continued and established the foundation for an empire that by 116 CE would encompass more than 6.5 million square miles (16.8 million sq. km) under the emperor Trajan. At this time the empire covered the full perimeter of the Mediterranean Sea, stretching north to Scotland, south to Arabia, and east to Mesopotamia.

Few Westerners today, be they from the Americas, Russia, or Europe, misinterpret the meaning of the nouns "czar," "kaiser," or "caesar," the last being the Latin root of the first two words, as well as the name of the man many deem the most famous in history. Napoleon and the Duke of Wellington both carried copies of Caesar's *Commentaries* on their campaigns, and their engagement at the Battle of Waterloo in 1815 was compared to that of Scipio and Hannibal at the Battle of Zama in 202 BCE.

Parallels such as these have been drawn regularly over the centuries. George Washington has been compared to Cincinnatus, and Theodore Roosevelt has been compared to Tiberius Gracchus. In an essay published in 1909, Consuelo Vanderbilt, the Duchess of Marlborough, likened the suffragist Christabel Pankhurst to Hortensia, daughter of the famous republican orator Hortensius. Hortensia followed in her father's footsteps and delivered a speech to the members of the Second Triumvirate in 42 BCE that succeeded in gaining a reduction in taxes on wealthy women.

British statesmen such as Winston Churchill and Harold Macmillan were steeped in Roman history. Churchill said he had "devoured" Edward Gibbon's *Decline and Fall of the Roman Empire* as a young man. In 1995, U.S. Senator Robert C. Byrd (who celebrated 50 years of service in the Senate in 2009) published his thoughts on the Roman senate's actions during the years of the republic. Nineteenth- and twentieth-century historical and cultural studies are couched in references to "America's Rome" and "Britain's Greece," and those ideas in turn refer back to assumptions and conclusions formed during the Renaissance and Middle Ages concerning Roman civilization.

Popular culture has its own adaptations of Roman history that are enjoyed the world over. Visual interpretations are especially popular as widespread interest in films such as William

Wyler's *Ben-Hur* (1959), Federico Fellini's *Satyricon* (1969), and Ridley Scott's *Gladiator* (2000), as well as the HBO television series *Rome* (2005–2007), attests. The comic book series *Astérix*, concerning the adventures of a proto-French hero who fights against Caesar's assaults on Gaul around 50 BCE, debuted more than 50 years ago (in 1959), and the 34th volume of *Astérix* was published in 2009.

In 12 chapters, *Ancient Rome: An Illustrated History* takes the student through the basics: Rome's origins and its early period of monarchy, the rise of the republic to the heights of its empire, and its subsequent transformation from pagan polytheism to Christianity. The volume is illustrated with strategically placed maps, time lines listing key dates and events, boxed sections of text for elaboration, and color photographs depicting various ancient artifacts as well as relevant images from the Renaissance and more recent times. Students will come away with specific knowledge that will help them understand the roots of modern institutions such as the current calendar, the development of spectator sports, and the origin of the Romance languages. It is no exaggeration to say that the history of Rome has served for better or for worse as a metaphor and reference point for world history. With that in mind, let us follow Augustine's famous imperatives: "Tolle et lege." Take up this book and read!

Michele Ronnick

Michele Ronnick is president of the Classical Association of the Middle West and South and a professor in the Department of Classical and Modern Languages, Literatures, and Cultures at Wayne State University, Detroit, MI.

Additional related information is available in the 11-volume *History of the Ancient and Medieval World*, second edition, and the corresponding online *Ancient and Medieval World* database at www.marshallcavendishdigital.com.

EARLY ROME

A ccording to legend, the city of Rome was ruled by seven kings, before the last of the line, Tarquin the Proud, was deposed. Rome then became a republic governed by a variety of assemblies and elected officials.

The early history of Rome is shrouded in mystery. The origins of the city are the subject of many myths, which have become inextricably interwoven with historical fact. Several of these stories promoted the idea that the Trojans were the ancestors of the Romans. These myths were gathered together and embellished by the Roman poet Virgil (70–19 BCE) in his epic poem the *Aeneid*. Other stories regarding the founding of Rome by the twins Romulus and Remus were relayed by the later writers Livy (59 BCE–17 CE) and Plutarch (c. 46–120 CE).

The origins of Rome

According to legend, the story of the founding of Rome begins with the fall of another great ancient city, Troy. After Troy's destruction, the Trojan hero Aeneas escaped with a small group of followers, eventually managing to reach the coast of Italy, where he landed on the estuary of the Tiber River and made a new home. He married a local princess, and their son, Ascanius, founded the city of Alba Longa on a site just southeast of present-day Rome. Ascanius's descendants reigned there for 14 generations, until the ruling king Numitor was dethroned by his brother Amulius.

Amulius arranged for Numitor's daughter, Rea Silvia, to become one of the Vestal Virgins (see box, page 9), the priestesses who tended the sacred hearth of the goddess Vesta. They were all forbidden to indulge in sexual intercourse. Nevertheless, Rea Silvia was seduced by Mars, the god of war, and gave birth to twin boys in the sanctuary of Vesta. When the children were discovered, Amulius threw Rea Silvia into a dungeon and had the infants put in a wicker basket and set adrift on the river. The basket became caught in the bulrushes, where the babies were suckled by a she-wolf until they were found by a shepherd. He took the twins home, adopted them, and named them Romulus and Remus.

When the twins reached adulthood, they met up with the deposed King Numitor and, through a series of coincidences, discovered their true origin. Romulus and Remus then initiated a revolution in Alba Longa, and Amulius was killed. Eager to found their own city, the brothers retreated with other pioneers into the Tiber hills, around 12 miles (19 km) to the northwest.

Before starting to build, Romulus and Remus decided to consult the augurs (priests who interpreted the wishes of the gods) to determine which brother would be king of the new city. However, when the augurs presented their conclusions, a fight broke out, and Romulus killed his brother.

So, according to tradition, Romulus became the first king of Rome, founding the city in 753 BCE. Legend also has it that he marked out the city's boundaries by plowing a furrow around the site, using a bronze plow pulled by a white ox and a white cow. In this way, he demarcated the sacred precinct called the *pomerium* and the Palatine Hill.

The rape of the Sabine women

The city of Rome prospered, but its population consisted only of men. To overcome this problem, Romulus attempted to persuade the neighboring Sabines to allow some of their women to marry Roman men. The Sabines refused, however. Romulus was forced to devise a cunning strategy. He invited all the Sabines to attend a religious celebration. The Sabines eagerly accepted the invitation, bringing their families along to enjoy the festivities. At Romulus's signal, every Roman seized and abducted a Sabine woman.

This act led to a savage war, in which the Sabines tried to win back their kidnapped women. Eventually, however, the Sabine women themselves pleaded for the two sides to be reconciled, to stop the bloodshed. The Romans and the Sabines agreed to form a single state, which was jointly ruled by Romulus and the Sabine leader, Titus Tatius. Romulus

This bronze statue, known as the Capitoline Wolf, was made by the Etruscans in the early fifth century BCE. The suckling infants, representing the twins Romulus and Remus, were added around 2,000 years later.

7

THE ROMAN WORLD

KEY

Roman territory
in 500 BCE

✗ Major battle

survived Tatius and ruled until 715 BCE, when, according to legend, he was taken up to heaven in a chariot driven by his father, Mars.

The early kings of Rome

The tale of Romulus and Remus is almost certainly purely mythical, but from this point of the story onward, some historical facts may start to be mixed in with the fiction. After the disappearance of Romulus, Numa Pompilius was elected king by the senate (a council of wise men). He was a priest-

ly king who established many of the Roman religious institutions. Numa Pompilius was said to have been instructed by a wood nymph with whom he held regular conversations. His peaceful reign was in contrast to that of his successor, the belligerent Tullus Hostilius, who ruled from 673 to 642 BCE and is thought to have destroyed Alba Longa. Tullus also founded the Curia Hostilia, an early meeting place of the senate.

Hostilius was succeeded in 641 BCE by the fourth king of Rome, Ancus Marcius, who was a grandson of Numa

THE VESTAL VIRGINS

The Vestal Virgins were six priestesses whose main function was to keep alight the eternal flame that burned in the public shrine of the goddess Vesta. Vesta was the goddess who presided over hearth and home, and every Roman family made offerings to her at mealtimes. Every city also had a public hearth, kept in a temple dedicated to Vesta. The fire in this hearth was never allowed to go out; it was the symbol of the city's spiritual heart.

The Vestal Virgins were taken from patrician families and had to be between the ages of six and ten when they were selected. They each served for a total of 30 years—as a novice for the first 10 years, as a Vestal Virgin proper for the next 10 years, and then as a tutor to the novices for the final 10 years.

The Vestal Virgins had to take a vow of chastity, and if this vow was broken, the punishment was severe; the offender was buried alive. However, if a Vestal Virgin survived her 30-year term of service, she was released from her duties and permitted to marry.

This mural from the first century CE depicts the wounded hero Aeneas, whose followers were believed to be the ancestors of the Romans.

Pompilius. Ancus Marcius ruled until 616 BCE and is famous for a bridge, the Pons Sublicius, that he had built across the Tiber River. A notable conqueror, he seized a number of Latin towns and moved their inhabitants to Rome.

The Etruscan kings

The first civilization on the Italian Peninsula had been established by the Etruscans (see box, page 13) and was centered on Etruria (roughly present-day Tuscany). According to tradition, the last three kings of Rome were Etruscans. The first of these Etruscan kings was Lucius Tarquinius Priscus. Legend has it that he was the son of a Corinthian nobleman, Demaratus, who had immigrated to the Etruscan city of Tarquinii. Tarquinius Priscus, however, decided to move to Rome with his wife Tanaquil. As they approached Rome, the story goes, a screaming eagle swooped down and seized the cap from Tanaquil's head. Tarquinius Priscus interpreted this as a favorable omen. Once established in

9

Rome, he quickly acquired a reputation as a notable citizen.

After the death of Ancus Marcius in 616 BCE, Tarquinius Priscus was crowned king. Rome prospered under his reign. During this time, he was responsible for the construction of a number of public buildings. Tarquinius Priscus is also said to have initiated the Roman Games and to have constructed a drainage system in the city. His conquests of neighboring peoples added considerably to the population.

Tarquinius Priscus died in 575 BCE during a palace revolt. He was replaced by a favorite of his wife Tanaquil—Servius Tullius. A man of obscure descent, Servius had previously been the head of Tanaquil's household and proved to be an able king. He created new classes of citizens and built a new fortified wall to protect the city. Later generations of Romans were to honor him as their favorite king, and they believed they owed many of their political institutions to him.

Servius was murdered in 534 BCE by his son-in-law and successor, Tarquinius Superbus (commonly known as either Tarquin the Proud or Tarquin the Younger). Tarquin, who was either the son or grandson of Tarquinius Priscus, seized the throne, murdered many supporters of the previous king, and proceeded to rule as a tyrant. He surrounded himself with a

This statue from the 17th century CE depicts the Trojan hero Aeneas carrying his aged father Anchises.

personal guard, pronounced judgments at random, and ignored political institutions. Tarquin distracted the people with military adventures and monumental construction projects. He is famous for having built a temple to Jupiter on the Capitoline Hill and paving the major streets of the city with blocks of granite. He is also credited with building the city's first public sewers, including the great Cloaca Maxima, which still function today.

However, in spite of these achievements, the people of Rome were not prepared to tolerate such an oppressive government. The crisis came in 510 BCE when Tarquin's son Sextus raped Lucretia, the wife of his own kinsman; Lucretia later committed suicide. Tarquin's crime provided a focus for dissent, which surfaced soon afterward when a number of leading aristocrats, led by Lucius Junius Brutus, another distant relative of the king, rose up in revolt against the tyrant. Tarquin and his family fled from the city, and although he later tried to reclaim the throne, all his efforts failed. The people of Rome subsequently turned their backs on monarchy as a system of government; from that moment on, the Romans would always abhor the basic idea of kingship—the words *king* and *tyrant* became virtually synonymous in Latin. Instead, the power was placed in the hands of the senate and a number of elected officials.

Latium

The semimythical account of the early years of Rome left by poets such as Livy and Plutarch is not the only source of information about Rome's development. Archaeologists and linguists have been able to piece together a parallel history of Rome that is more firmly based on historical fact. They have established that the plain lying between the Tiber River and the Apennine Hills was once populated by people who called their land Latium, and themselves Latini, or Latins.

The Latins were probably descended from a people who invaded Italy during the course of the second millennium BCE. These people spoke an Indo-European language and held elaborate funeral ceremonies, in which they cremated the bodies of their dead. The old-est settlement associated with this culture that has been excavated dates from the 16th century BCE.

Shortly after 1000 BCE, other population groups appeared. In contrast to their predecessors, they buried their dead. It is possible that these groups were related to the Sabines of legend. They were also an Indo-European people who spoke a Latin dialect. It is evident that, between 900 and 600 BCE, many Latin settlements existed, each with its own funeral customs.

Until the end of the seventh century BCE, Latium remained an underdeveloped rural area. The Latins lived in small hilltop villages, which may have been surrounded by wooden palisades. Their primitive huts were made of twigs sealed with pitch and had only two openings, a

This fresco from the14th century CE depicts the execution of Rea Silvia, the mother of Romulus and Remus.

11

This painting, by French artist Jacques-Louis David (1748–1825 CE), depicts the Sabine women and their children attempting to intercede in the battle between their own soldiers and their Roman abductors.

door and a hole in the roof to let out smoke. Urns shaped like these huts have been found holding cremation ashes.

From the late seventh century BCE onward, the area started to develop. Latium was in contact with some highly sophisticated cultures—the Etruscans to the north, the Greek colonies to the south, and Carthage, whose sailors regularly visited the coast. From the politically dominant Etruscans, the Latins acquired technical skills, artistic styles, and political and religious practices. As the popplation of Latium grew, farmland became scarce. To increase the area of viable agricultural land, dams and waterworks were built, some of which still survive. The hill villages gradually evolved into *oppida* (small fortified city-states), and

the *oppida* formed themselves into federations, which originally had only a religious purpose but in the end became political as well.

The birth of Rome

Around 625 BCE, political unity among the *oppida*-dwellers gave rise to a city the size of Romulus's *pomerium* in the valley between the Palatine Hill and the Capitoline Hill. The city, called Roma (a name of Etruscan origin), was initially ruled by kings. The *rex*, or king, performed the function of supreme judge, high priest, and commander-in-chief of the army, and he led his army in person. The king was advised (on his request) by a council of elders known as the senate, which also chose his successor. The

THE ETRUSCANS

The Etruscans were a people who occupied the area of central Italy that is now Tuscany from around 900 BCE. No one is quite sure where they came from. One theory—the autochthonous theory—suggests that they were the descendants of the earliest known population of north and central Italy—the Villanovans. Another theory suggests that the Etruscans were immigrants who came from western Anatolia. The fifth-century-BCE Greek historian Herodotus maintained that the Etruscans were descended from the Tyrrhenians, who had come from the east via Lydia, and this theory is borne out by the fact that many of the Etruscans' characteristics, such as their religious customs, seem to have eastern origins.

Wherever they came from, the Etruscans established a distinct culture that flourished from the beginning of the seventh century BCE. They had their own unique language, but their culture showed much Greek influence. They adopted many Greek myths and legends, and because they imported many Greek vases, their potters soon began imitating Greek ceramics. In the seventh century BCE, the Etruscans adopted the Greek alphabet.

Etruscan cities were carefully laid out and enclosed by a *pomerium* (sacred boundary). Later cities were laid out on a grid system. The temple occupied a special area. The front of the temple had two rows of columns—a feature of the so-called Tuscan style of architecture. Houses were built of sun-dried mud bricks and were either simple rectangular two-story dwellings or based on a more sophisticated design that consisted of a set of rooms arranged around a central courtyard. Originally, each city was ruled by a king, but in the fifth century BCE, the kings were replaced almost everywhere by governments of aristocrats.

Not a great deal is known about the Etruscan religion. However, one aspect of it did involve a process of divination by studying the internal organs of sacrificial animals. While the functions of many of the Etruscan gods are not known, their deities often resembled the gods of Greece and Rome; for example, their goddess Menerva was closely related to the Greek goddess of wisdom, Athena, and her Roman counterpart, Minerva.

The Etruscans were traders and conducted much of their commerce by sea. They exported materials such as iron ore, which was mined on the island of Elba, and craft items made from bronze and gold. In return, they imported exotic goods from Africa and craft items from mainland Greece.

The height of Etruscan power came in the sixth and fifth centuries BCE. Thereafter, their influence declined, and they came under frequent attack from Greeks, Latins, Romans, and Gauls. After Etruria was seized by the Romans, the Etruscan language gradually disappeared. Eventually, by the first century BCE, the Etruscans had been totally absorbed into the Roman culture.

This bronze Etruscan statuette of a warrior dates to between 420 and 400 BCE. Its style is influenced by Greek sculpture.

According to legend, Numa Pompilius was the second king of Rome. He is depicted here in a 16th-century-CE woodcut.

beians were generally peasants and had little political power. This class distinction probably originated during the time of the monarchy, but it gained far greater political significance after the last king was deposed.

In Rome at this time, the head of a family wielded particular power. He was called the *pater* (father), and his authority over his wife, children (whatever their age), and slaves was initially absolute. A Roman *pater* had the right to kill his wife or sell his child as a slave without breaking the law. Fathers who were related and bore the same family name formed a *gens* (clan). In the beginning, the king ruled the clans through the senate, which was composed of the fathers of prominent families. It is likely that the fathers who sat on the council began to distinguish themselves from the family heads who did not.

The patricians comprised the *populus* (people), from which the army was originally drawn. The king called out the *populus* as needed and then led the army himself, preceded by his guards (called lictors) bearing the fasces. The fasces symbolized the king's regal and later magisterial authority and consisted of cylindrical bundles of wooden rods wrapped around an ax and tied tightly together. The fasces symbolized unity as well as power. Servius Tullius is usually credited with a major reform that permitted plebeians, who by that time could hold property and wealth, to serve in the army. They were assigned to a rank in accordance with their wealth.

Class struggle

The class struggle that characterized the patrician–plebeian relationship was central to Roman social history and the development of government organizations. Gradually, the social and political barriers against the plebeians were eroded, but for a long time, the plebeians

senate's nomination was accepted or rejected by acclamation in a public meeting or an army assembly. The *populus* (people) were also consulted in matters of war and peace.

Before the Etruscan domination of Rome, the monarchy is thought to have been largely ceremonial. Under the Etruscans, it assumed greater importance, but by 509 BCE, the Romans had put an end to both Etruscan power and the monarchy itself.

Roman society

In early Rome, there were two social classes, excluding slaves. These classes were the *patricii* (patricians), who originally were the only ones with political rights, and the other free Romans, the *plebes* (the masses, or plebeians). The plecontinued to exist as a separate and subordinate class. Marriages between patricians and plebeians were not recognized by law, and the children of such marriages lost their patrician status.

The patricians formed only a small minority of the free population, however. The fact that they managed to keep power in their own hands for as long as they did was largely due to an important social institution called the *clientela* (client system). Under this system, it was customary for free but powerless citizens to bind themselves to a powerful man of the patrician class. These people were called *clientes* and may originally have been tenants of the patrician, but as time went on, this was not always the case. The *patrones* (patron) could demand obedience and service from the *clientes*, but the bond of the *clientela* had mutual benefits. It was the patron's duty to help the *clientes* in time of need, if they were involved in a lawsuit, for example.

The early republic

Once the kings were driven out of Rome, the city became a republic, meaning a state governed by the people. In practice, however, the government

This 16th-century-CE painting by Perino del Vaga depicts Tarquin the Proud founding the Temple of Jupiter on the Capitoline Hill.

THE LARES

Among the most important gods worshipped by the Romans were the Lares, protective spirits who presided over a number of different areas. For example, the *Lares viales* looked after people traveling by road, while the *Lares permarini* watched over seafarers. For most Romans, however, the most important Lar was the *Lar familiaris*, the family Lar.

The *Lar familiaris* was unusual in that he was seen as an individual figure when most Lares were worshipped as pairs of twins. He was worshipped in the home, often at a shrine that took the form of a miniature temple. The *Lar familiaris* was believed to live in the house itself, watching over successive generations. Lares were often represented by figurines of dancing youths.

Rome's position on the Tiber River linked the city to the port of Ostia, and the connection facilitated Rome's development as a city.

largely lay in the hands of the patricians. A great deal of the power resided in the senate. Just as it had previously elected the king for life from the patrician class, the senate now chose two chief executives to serve on an annual basis. Originally called praetors (leaders) and selected exclusively from among the patricians, these executives were later given the title of consul.

To some extent, the praetors inherited the power and pomp of the kings. They wore the royal purple on their togas and were preceded on ceremonial occasions by the lictors and fasces. They led the army to war and wielded absolute power over the citizens. However, as each praetor had the power of veto over decisions made by the other, neither had the kind of autocratic authority once held by the king. Furthermore, their power was limited by the fact that their term of office ended after one year.

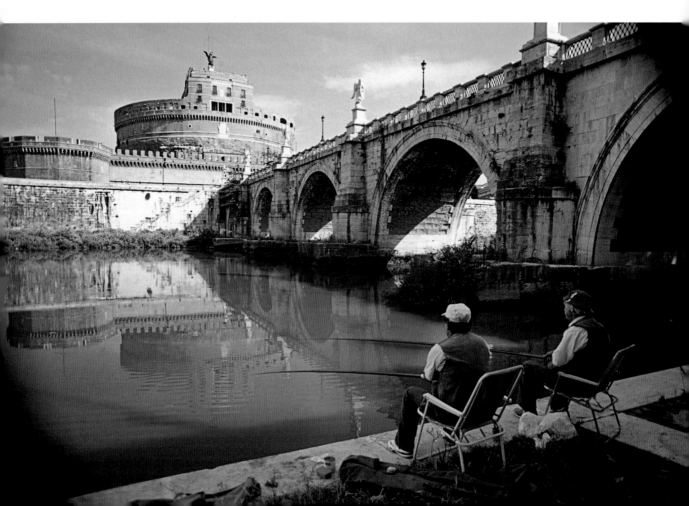

The senate and other assemblies

Much of the real power in the republic resided in the senate. The members of this assembly were drawn from a few leading patrician families. These *patres* were lifetime members, and their senate seats passed to their heirs as an inherited right. Under the monarchy, the mass of the plebeians were unrepresented in the government, but in the days of the republic, a second group of senators, drawn from the plebeians, was appointed. These senators were called the *conscripti* (enrolled), and the senators as a whole were called the *patres et conscripti*. Although the *conscripti* also held the office for life, they could not pass it on to their descendants.

The early republic also inherited a popular assembly from the time of the monarchy. The *comitia curiata* was originally made up of *curiae* (clubs) of warriors. The number of *curiae* was fixed at 30. Under the monarchy, the chief function of the *comitia curiata* was to confirm the election of a king. Over time, the assembly's meetings became purely ceremonial, and by the time of the republic, its function had dwindled, so that just 30 individuals, each representing a single *curia*, were required to invest the praetors after an election.

The *comitia centuriata*

During the sixth century BCE, Rome had adopted the Greek mode of warfare, using a phalanx of heavily armed foot soldiers who fought in close formation, protected by large shields and using thrusting spears. Armor was expensive, and service in the Roman army was reserved for those who could afford to pay for their own military equipment. For this reason, Servius Tullius had conducted a census to determine the property of every citizen. Wealth, measured almost exclusively in terms of land, became the sole criterion for enlistment.

This shrine to household gods was found in the city of Pompeii.

Every year a *legio* (military conscription or draft) was drawn from those deemed able to afford military service. Each group of 100 men was referred to as a *centuria* (century), and from these annual conscriptions, a new kind of popular assembly developed—the *comitia centuriata*. The *comitia curiata* gradually lost its position to this new assembly, which consisted of serving soldiers and veterans.

The *comitia centuriata* met on the Campus Martius (Field of Mars) outside the city's *pomerium*. The assembly included 30 centuries of men called *juniores* (juniors), who were between the ages of 17 and 46. Another 30 centuries were composed of *seniores* (seniors)—citizens who were too old to fight but who retained the right to vote. These 60

This urn in the shape of a hut was made by people of the Villanovan culture, who were predecessors of the Romans and lived in central Italy.

By the third century BCE, there were six separate property classes in the *comitia centuriata*. The first class consisted of 18 centuries of *equites* and 80 centuries of juniors and seniors. The second, third, and fourth classes contained 20 centuries each, while the fifth class consisted of 30 centuries. There were also five additional centuries that were reserved for non-combatants, such as trumpeters and armorers. In all, the army was composed of 193 centuries.

The *comitia centuriata* had the power to decide whether Rome should go to war or not. It also elected magistrates, acted as a high court, and had some powers to legislate. Despite the addition of representatives of the poorer sections of society, the assembly was still dominated by the wealthy. The method of voting was not "one man, one vote"; it was by centuries. The votes of the 18 cavalry units were taken first, followed by those of the 80 first-class centuries. Voting halted as soon as a majority had been reached. If the first-class centuries voted as a bloc, then the centuries from the lower classes would not even get a chance to vote.

The rise of the plebeians

The plebeians never formed a homogeneous group, either economically or culturally. There were poor plebeians, middle-class plebeians, and wealthy plebeians. The ambitions of the poorest were limited to owning a piece of land and to seeing the revocation of the strict debt law that could have a debtor sold into slavery. The richest plebeians, however, had political ambitions. They wanted a share of the power and the privileges of the patricians. Many of the most respectable plebeians came from regions that had been conquered by Rome; these men had held prominent positions at home and wanted comparable status in their new place of residence.

centuries of foot soldiers, together with 18 centuries of cavalry (*equites*), formed a propertied class that excluded citizens who were too poor to afford army service and were thus unable to vote.

By the end of the fifth century BCE, the number of Roman citizens had increased to such an extent that 40, rather than 30, centuries of juniors were regularly recruited. The legion also expanded to take in less heavily armed soldiers, who did not need to have as much property to qualify for army service. The army was thus divided into two separate classes.

Things came to a head in 494 BCE, when there was a mass exodus of plebeians from Rome. According to legend, they withdrew to a nearby mountain, where they formed an assembly called the *concilium plebis* (council of plebeians) and threatened to found a separate city if the patricians refused to recognize their assembly and the officials it chose. These officials were called the *tribuni plebis* (tribunes of the plebeians). Eventually, the plebeians were persuaded to return to Rome, and two tribunes of the plebeians were recognized. These two tribunes became spokesmen for the plebeian cause and could intervene if a plebeian was in danger of being punished unjustly. The tribunes could also override the decisions of the magistrates by uttering the single word *veto* (I forbid).

The number of tribunes of the plebeians was gradually increased to 10. The plebeians declared their tribunes to be inviolable, which meant that anyone attempting to arrest or intimidate them could be killed. Soon after the tribunes of the plebeians were officially sanctioned, an assembly of plebeians, called the *concilium plebis tributum*, started to be held, and in 471 BCE, it also received official recognition.

Another important victory was won by the plebeians in 445 BCE. The introduction of the Canuleian Law repealed the prohibition on marriages between patricians and plebeians and declared intermarriage to be legal. This move meant that rich plebeian families could now enter into alliances with patricians, a change that was bound to have long-term political consequences.

This bronze mirror was made by the Etruscans, who were known as skilled metalworkers.

The *comitia tributa*

By the middle of the fifth century BCE, a new popular assembly had been formed. This new body was the *comitia tributa* (assembly of the districts), which was set up on the model of the *concilium plebis* but was an assembly of all classes of citizens, plebeians and patricians alike. Votes were taken by tribes, or districts, just as they were taken by centuries in the *comitia curiata*. However, no distinctions were made among the districts, while within each district, the principle of "one man, one vote" was upheld.

Over the years, Rome had grown too big to be governed by just two chief officials. For some time, the consuls had been appointing assistants, called quaestors, to handle some criminal cases. The quaestors were junior magistrates, and after 447 BCE, two were appointed annually by the *comitia tributa*. Soon afterwards, two additional quaestors were put in charge of public finances. From 421 BCE, the office was open to plebeians as well as patricians.

Another position to be established in the fifth century BCE was that of the *aedile* (temple functionary). This position was another official magistracy to which plebeians could be elected. There were originally two *aediles*, who were connected with an important plebeian cult center—a temple on the Aventine Hill dedicated to Ceres, the goddess of agriculture, and Liber and Libera, a pair of fertility and cultivation deities. The *aediles* had considerable economic power. As state officials, they were in charge of a number of public works, the public food supply, and the markets.

This wall painting from an Etruscan tomb depicts servants and musicians. It dates to the first half of the fifth century BCE.

The number of magistracies that could be held by plebeians increased steadily over the years. However, the most important post—that of consul—remained in the hands of the patricians.

Legal protection

An important milestone in the evolving constitution of ancient Rome was the setting up in 451 BCE of a special commission of 10 learned men known as the *decemvirs* (decemvirate or 10 men). This move followed prolonged agitation on the part of the plebeians for the laws of Rome to be defined and written down, mainly to avoid arbitrary punishments being meted out by patrician magistrates. The task of the decemvirate was to record all common law and to define the penalties for breaking it. The resulting compilation was known as the Laws of the Twelve Tables, because the laws were engraved on 12 bronze tablets that were placed in the forum.

From that point on, the patrician magistrates could no longer make legal decisions at their own whim; they had to make their judgments in accordance with this formal standard. In theory, the tables granted equal rights to all free citizens, but in practice, the weak and vulnerable still had to rely on powerful patrons for protection or legal redress.

The Licinian-Sextian Laws

A further development in the struggle of the plebeians for political power was the introduction of a new office, that of military tribune with consular power, in 445 BCE. While the senate refused to allow a plebeian to act as consul, a plebeian could be elected as a military tribune. From 445 BCE onward, either two consuls or two military tribunes were elected each year. This practice continued until 367 BCE, when two tribunes, Licinius and Sextius, presented a bill to the *comitia tributa* proposing that the annual consulship should be restored and that one of the two consuls should be plebeian. The following year, Sextius became the first plebeian consul.

The same year, another new official appeared: the praetor. The praetor was a consular deputy and was primarily concerned with the administration of justice, but he could also take command of an army. Like the consuls, the praetor was elected by the *comitia centuriata*, the old military assembly. For 20 years, the office remained in the hands of the patricians, but in 337 BCE, the first plebeian was elected praetor.

In 356 BCE, a plebeian, Marcius Rutilus, was appointed dictator. The role of dictator had been established at the

THE LAWS OF THE TWELVE TABLES

The Laws of the Twelve Tables were established in 451 BCE after plebeian agitation for a formal code of law. A decemvirate, or committee of 10, was given the task of setting down the common law of Rome in clear terms. The resulting legal code covered both public and private life and reflected the patriarchal nature of the society for which it was written. The code covered family law, property rights and inheritance, debt, funeral rites, legal processes, and offenses against the community.

As far as family law was concerned, the code confirmed the almost unlimited authority of the *pater familias* (father of the family). He had the power of life and death over his wife, children, slaves, and plebeian clients, although he was obliged to call a family council before making a life-and-death decision. The position of women in society was completely subordinate to that of men. A woman was subject to her father before marriage and to her husband after marriage. If a woman became a widow, she was put in the charge of a male relative.

Crimes against private property attracted severe punishments. A person whose property had been stolen had the right to put the thief to

death. Reflecting the importance of the food supply, agriculture was given special protection. Anyone who maliciously set fire to another's crops could be burned alive. A debtor who could not pay his debts was regarded as a criminal; his creditor could put him to death or sell him as a slave.

These laws reflected the society's predominant interest in possessions. Other provisions were more enlightened. For example, one law stipulated that a marriage could be ended by mutual consent; if a wife absented herself from the marital bed for three nights and declared herself unwilling to return, the marriage could be dissolved. Also stipulated in family law was the obligation of a father to give his sons (but not his daughters) a good education.

The Twelve Tables contain little legislation with regard to politics. However, the code did allow citizens to appeal to the popular assembly about decisions made against them in the courts. These laws were never formally abolished, and because they were written in Latin, they provided a foretaste of the use of Latin as the language of the legal profession throughout Europe.

beginning of the fifth century BCE, when military emergencies made it imperative for one man to have absolute control of the armed forces. It was a command that lasted for six months only, and during that time, everyone was subject to the authority of the dictator.

In 351 BCE, a plebeian was elected to the office of censor for the first time. This was a relatively new office, to which two men were elected every five years. The censors were responsible for conducting the census and registering new members of the senate. Censors could also expel unworthy senators, making the office one of great significance and prestige.

The empowerment of the plebeians brought about a rapid change in the composition of the senate, which by the end of the fourth century BCE had

In this 18th-century-CE illustration, a Roman lictor carries the fasces, an ax contained within a bundle of sticks.

The Circus Maximus was used for chariot races in the early republic.

become predominantly plebeian. This development improved the senate's relationship with the *concilium plebis*, which was still a purely plebeian assembly. This body elected the tribunes of the people and passed resolutions that officially related only to the plebeians, but in practice affected everyone.

End of the class struggle

In 287 BCE, a historic law was enacted. The *lex Hortensia*, named after the plebeian dictator Hortensius, stipulated that a decree of the plebeian assembly should have the same effect in law as a decree of either of the other two assemblies, the *comitia centuriata* and the *comitia tributa*. This law was a major step in the class struggle and greatly increased the power of the richer plebeians. The poorer plebeians also had cause for satisfaction, because over the course of the fourth century BCE, the cruel debt law had been modified. A debtor could no longer be sold as a slave, and land was now regularly distributed among the less well-to-do Romans.

The beginning of the third century BCE saw a new elite emerging in Roman society—the *nobiles* (nobles). These people were a mixture of patricians and plebeians who had held the highest office (the consulate), or whose fathers or forefathers had done so. This new hereditary ruling class of *nobilitas* (nobility) controlled the senate and, thanks to their array of clients and their own prestige, the popular assemblies as well. Once accorded little administrative authority, the senators now dominated government in both domestic matters and foreign affairs.

Senatorial power had increased with the power of Rome, and the struggle between patricians and plebeians seemed to be over, but Rome was never to become a true democracy. While 287 BCE saw the beginning of a period

of relatively harmonious cooperation among the highest circles of Roman society, the hardships of the poorest plebeians remained unaltered. Despite the comparative peace on the Italian Peninsula and unparalleled expansion abroad, the old class contest was to reemerge in the political arena as the aristocratic and populist parties fought for control.

The Curia in the Forum Romanum was the meeting place of the Roman senate.

See also:

Revolution and Reform (page 44) • Rome's Early Wars and Conquests (page 24)

ROME'S EARLY WARS AND CONQUESTS

In the late seventh century BCE, Rome was just a small settlement; by the late third century BCE, Rome was a major power that dominated almost all the Italian Peninsula. Success in battle was the key to this dramatic transformation.

In the seventh and sixth centuries BCE, Rome was just one of many hundreds of small towns and cities scattered over the Italian Peninsula. Rome lay between Latium and Etruria. At various times during the following years, Rome would either be ruled by the Etruscans or allied to the Latins.

Greek-Etruscan conflict

In the sixth century BCE, the major powers in Italy were the Etruscans, who were settled in the north of the country, and the various Greek colonies established in the south. The Etruscans ruled the territory between the valley of the Po River and Campania, while in the south their influence reached as far as the Bay of Naples.

The Greeks in the southern Italian Peninsula were constantly on a war footing with the Etruscans. Around 535 BCE, the Etruscans allied themselves with the powerful Carthaginians in order to dislodge the Greeks from Alalia, on the island of Corsica. Some years later, the tide turned against the Etruscans when an attack on the Greek port of Cumae failed. Around 506 BCE, an alliance of Latin cities, with the help of Cumae, defeated the Etruscans near Aricia, just south of Rome. The victory was an important symbol of the erosion of Etruscan power.

Legendary heroes

The legendary defeat of the Etruscans at Aricia was described by the first-century-BCE Greek historian Dionysius of Halicarnassus. His account placed the downfall of the Etruscans at roughly the same time that the traditional account of the founding of Rome placed the overthrow of Etruscan king Tarquin the Proud.

Other legends give further accounts of Roman resistance. One famous myth involved the Etruscan ruler Lars Porsena, who attempted to return the Tarquins to power in Rome. The Romans reputedly demonstrated great courage in the wars that followed. One hero, Horatius, single-handedly held back Porsena's forces while comrades pulled down a strategic bridge.

Another story concerning Porsena is that of Mucius Scaevola, who was captured during an attempt to kill Porsena. When brought before Porsena, Mucius placed his hand on live coals, to show that he was oblivious to pain and that the Romans would continue to resist however long the war endured. Porsena was so impressed that he supposedly ended his siege of the city.

Mucius Scaevola was just one of a number of semimythical heroes who were later seen as examples of the Roman characteristics of courage, selflessness, and patriotism. These qualities were also displayed by the Horatii, three

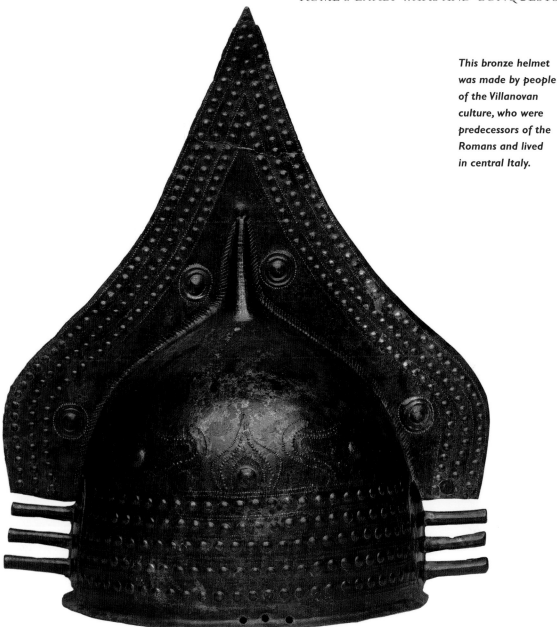

This bronze helmet was made by people of the Villanovan culture, who were predecessors of the Romans and lived in central Italy.

heroes from an earlier period of Rome's history. The Horatii were triplets who were said to have lived in the mid-seventh century BCE, when Rome was at war with the neighboring town of Alba Longa. It was agreed that the outcome of the war would be decided by a fight between the Horatii and the Curiatii, another set of triplets from Alba Longa. Two members of the Horatii were quickly killed. The third pretended to flee and was chased by the Curiatii. However, because the Curiatii had been injured, they became spread out, allowing the surviving member of the Horatii to kill them one by one. When the victorious Horatius returned to Rome, his sister, who had been betrothed to one of the Curiatii, burst into tears on hearing of her lover's death. Disgusted by her lack

ROMAN CHARACTER

Rome owed much of its success to the strength of its traditions, which lasted remarkably late into the imperial period and which combined to create a distinctly Roman identity.

Among the most important of these traditions was the determination never to be ruled by kings. Even during the empire, the forms of old Roman government were preserved. The standards carried by Roman legions in imperial times did not carry the emperor's name, but the letters SPQR, which stood for a phrase meaning "for the senate and people of Rome." Posts that originated during the republic, such as quaestor and consul, still had a meaning and a function hundreds of years later. Romans felt themselves part of a unique society, not subjects of a monarch.

Family life and family traditions were considered to lie at the very heart of Roman life, and the names of eminent families recur over the centuries in Roman history. It was very important for a man to gain success in war or civil life in order to add to the prestige of his family. The family and the home also played a central role in Roman religion.

Another key Roman characteristic was the way the city was implacable and unyielding toward its foes. Many enemies of Rome, particularly during the republic, beat the Romans in a battle, but few were able to defeat them in a war. The great heroes of Roman tradition were those who embodied this unyielding, granite-like attitude—men such as Cato the Elder, whose oft-repeated mantra was "Carthage must be destroyed."

Finally, the Roman system of government allowed ambitious men to succeed. During the republic, the consular system, in which two consuls served in partnership for a year, encouraged each consul to do what he could to make a success of his year in office. This arrangement often led to foolhardy mistakes, but it also contributed to great successes. In spite of attempts by patricians and senators to protect their position, the Roman system eventually allowed wider groups of people to participate in government and to achieve great success. Even during the empire, the net of power grew wider, as people from the provinces were able to take on major posts and even to become emperor.

of patriotism, Horatius killed her on the spot. He was condemned to death for the murder, but pardoned when he appealed to the Roman people. In later centuries, the story of the Horatii was told to underline the importance of selfless devotion to the Roman state.

Alliance and invasion

At the beginning of the fifth century BCE, Rome's ambitions to become the dominant city in Latium brought it into conflict with members of the Latin League. Around 496 BCE, the Romans defeated a Latin army in a battle near Lake Regillus. Shortly afterward, Rome and the league entered into an alliance in which the various towns and cities agreed to contribute to an army for mutual self-defense.

By the beginning of the fourth century BCE, Rome's main source of danger came from Celtic tribes who were streaming westward from central Europe. Around 390 BCE, a horde of Gauls swept through Etruria, and the city of Clusium asked Rome to come to its aid. Rome thought that the barbarians would be easily destroyed, but at the Allia River north of Rome, a Latin-Roman army was nearly annihilated. The defeat was so complete that most Romans abandoned Rome without further resistance. However, a few defenders took up a position on the Capitoline Hill, which, with its temple and fortress, was the only part of Rome that could be defended. From that vantage point, the Romans prepared themselves for a siege and watched as the Gauls burned the city to the ground.

The defense of the Capitoline Hill gave rise to many legends. According to one story, the Gauls tried to take the hill garrison by surprise, through a badly guarded entrance. However, the sacred geese in the temple warned the Romans of the attack with their honking. It is not clear whether the Capitoline Hill was ever taken. What is clear is that the Gauls were more interested in booty than conquest. They were eventually bought off with a payment of 1,000 troy pounds (375 kg) of gold.

In the end, the Gauls settled only in the northern Italian Peninsula, an area that the Romans did not consider part of the Italian Peninsula proper. They called it Gallia Cisalpina (Gaul on this side of the Alps) to distinguish it from Gallia Transalpina (Gaul across the Alps).

The defeat at the hands of the Gauls severely dented Rome's prestige. To protect themselves against future threat, the Romans reorganized their army and built a defensive stone wall, 24 feet (7 m) tall, around their city. However, for some time to come, it was not the Gauls they had to fear, but their neighbors in

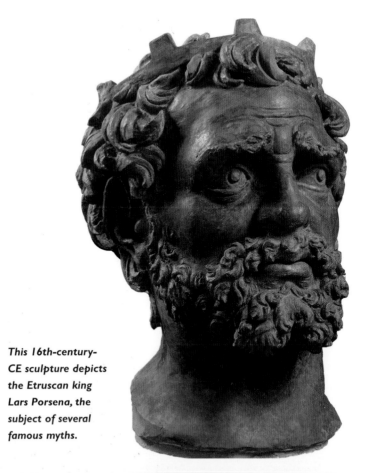

This 16th-century-CE sculpture depicts the Etruscan king Lars Porsena, the subject of several famous myths.

Mucius Scaevola thrusts his hand onto red-hot coals, impressing the Etruscan king Lars Porsena with his courage. Mucius became a hero to future Roman generations. This is a detail from an illustration in a 15th-century-CE copy of Dante's The Divine Comedy.

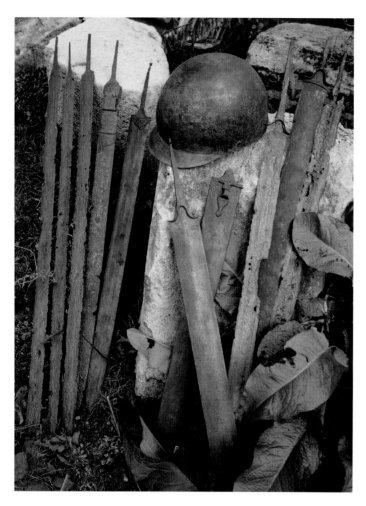

These iron swords and bronze helmets were made by the Celts and date to the third century BCE. A century earlier, a Celtic army had sacked Rome.

Apennines, the Latin cities supported Rome in repelling the invaders.

Rome came into conflict with the Samnites for the first time in 343 BCE. The rich city of Capua was being threatened by the Samnites and appealed to Rome for protection. Rome sent a large army, which succeeded in driving the Samnites from Campania. Immediately after the war, however, the Latin League rebelled once more against its Roman masters. The struggle continued for two years, but Rome, now allied with the Samnites, was ultimately successful in subduing the Latin resistance.

In 338 BCE, the Latin League was abolished, and Rome finally became the undisputed ruler of central Italy. A number of Latin cities became part of the Roman state, and in many cases, their citizens were awarded Roman citizenship. Other cities retained their independence but were still allied to Rome.

The Samnites did not remain allies of Rome for very long. Hostilities were resumed in 327 BCE and raged until 304 BCE. In 321 BCE, the consuls initiated an offensive campaign, marching an army of 20,000 men into Samnite territory. At the Caudine Forks (a narrow valley between two mountains), they were surrounded by Samnite warriors and forced to surrender after a few days of fighting. The captured consuls had to sign a peace treaty, awarding several Roman possessions to the Samnites. Before the army was allowed to retreat, it was subjected to the humiliation of passing under the yoke—a low gateway of enemy lances.

When the consuls returned to Rome, the treaty they had signed was rejected by the senate, and the war continued. Another consul was defeated by the Samnites in 309 BCE, after which the Romans changed their tactics. Instead of going on the offensive, they decided to await attack by the Samnites. This assault came in 305 BCE, when

Latium. After the Celtic invasion, a number of Latin cities rebelled against what they thought was a weaker Rome. It took decades of warfare for Rome to restore the supremacy that it had once enjoyed. However, in 358 BCE, following the defeat of the cities of Tibur and Praeneste, a new treaty was signed that established Rome as the head of a new Latin League, for a time at least

Wars against the Samnites

Although the Latins had few reasons to be satisfied with Roman rule, tribal interests had to be sacrificed when Latium was threatened from outside. During a war with the Samnites, warlike mountain tribes from the southern the Samnites invaded Campania. The Romans proved victorious in the ensuing campaign, and a year later, they made peace with the Samnites, putting Campania under permanent Roman control. Even so, hostilities were resumed in 298 BCE, and it took the Romans until 290 to eliminate the last Samnite threat in one final great war. Only the Greek colonies in the south of Italy remained independent of Rome.

Greek colonies and Pyrrhus

The Greek colonies could have been formidable enemies of Rome if they had acted in unison or if they had received assistance from their mother city-states in Greece. However, by the time Rome had defeated the Samnites, the mother cities had long since severed contact with their colonies in the Italian Peninsula. Therefore, the Greek colonies were forced to hire mercenary generals (who usually came from Greece) to command their armies.

This 18th-century-CE engraving depicts four Samnite warriors. The Samnites came from a mountainous region in central Italy and fought a series of wars with the Romans in the fourth and third centuries BCE.

Rome became involved with the Greek colonies when the Athenian colony of Thurii sought its support against the Lucanians. Soon, other Greek cities were asking for Rome's protection. This alarmed Tarentum, which was the richest and most powerful Greek city on the Italian Peninsula.

The inhabitants of Tarentum, who considered the Romans to be barbarians and believed that they should not meddle in Greek affairs, mobilized an army and drove off the Roman forces that had come to the assistance of Thurii. The Tarentans then hired a Greek general to command their army. Their choice was Pyrrhus, king of Epirus, a kingdom on the west coast of Greece.

Pyrrhus was an extremely ambitious warrior who dreamed of creating a large empire for himself. He gladly went to the aid of Tarentum, taking with him a highly disciplined army of 25,000 men and 20 elephants. When he arrived in Tarentum, he set himself up as a dictator.

He ordered the theaters and gymnasia to be closed and forced the citizens to eat military fare and engage in military exercises. These moves did not make him popular. However, Pyrrhus did succeed in saving the Tarentans from Rome, for a time at least.

Pyrrhic victories

The Romans fought hard against Pyrrhus, yet he twice emerged victorious—at the Battle of Heraclea in 280 BCE and at the Battle of Asculum in 279 BCE. At both battles, the Romans put up fierce resistance, and the Greeks suffered heavy losses. Pyrrhus is reputed to have exclaimed, "One more victory like that and I will be lost!" The battles ensured that Pyrrhus's name would remain famous; a victory that proves so costly as to be tantamount to a defeat is still known as a Pyrrhic victory.

At one point, when Rome was ready to make peace with Pyrrhus, a former censor, Appius Claudius, paralyzed and blind, was brought into the senate in a sedan chair. He told the assembly that he had never reconciled himself to being blind, but he would now prefer to be deaf as well, so he might not hear the terms of the disgraceful treaty that Rome was about to conclude. The senate was so impressed by his words that the treaty talks with Pyrrhus were called off.

After the heavy losses incurred in his two victories, and his failure to secure a peace treaty with the Romans, Pyrrhus withdrew his forces from southern Italy and transferred his attentions to Sicily. There, he scored great successes against the Carthaginians, who were the dominant power on the island. However, during Pyrrhus's three-year absence from Italy, the Romans drove the Tarentans

THE ROMAN ARMY

Rome's successful conquests in the late fourth century and early third century BCE depended to a large extent on its highly trained and highly disciplined army. Early in the fourth century BCE, the army was radically reorganized, following the disastrous defeat by the Gauls at the Battle of Allia in 390 BCE.

In the early fifth century BCE, the Roman legion had consisted of 3,000 heavily armed foot soldiers. Over the course of the fourth century BCE, this was increased to 6,000 heavy infantry troops and 2,400 light infantry. In 366 BCE, the annual draft was split between the two consuls, each commanding a legion of 4,200 men. During the great war with the Samnites, this annual draft was doubled to four legions, two for each consul, reflecting the growth in Rome's population. The legion still comprised lines of heavily and less heavily armed soldiers.

By the third century BCE, the armament had become generally uniform. It consisted of a bronze helmet, a scutum (large leather-covered shield), two javelins, and a sword. Wealthier soldiers also had a metal cuirass, a piece of armor covering the back and the chest. The sons of senators and of a growing number of wealthy citizens who were not senators served in the cavalry—200 to 300 men in each legion.

The Romans borrowed the organizing principle of the maniple from the Samnites, and this resulted in greater flexibility on the battlefield. Under this system, the legion was divided into three lines, with the youngest soldiers at the front. Each line was not solid, but consisted of maniples (rectangular groups) of 120 soldiers with spaces between them. Soldiers from the rear could come up through the gaps in the lines to present a solid front when necessary.

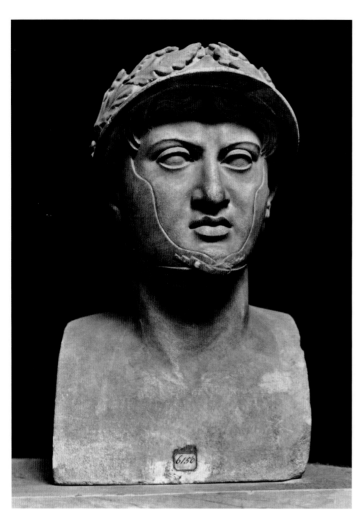

This bust depicts the Greek mercenary general Pyrrhus, who fought several battles against Roman forces in the third century BCE.

Rome. Rome had not always been successful in battle in the preceding centuries, but it always continued the struggle, even after defeat on the battlefield. Roman armaments and tactics were constantly being improved and, to some degree, would be adapted according to the opponents faced by the army.

When the Romans conquered a city, they sometimes razed it and enslaved its citizens. More often, however, the city and its people would be incorporated into the Roman state. In this way, the number of Roman civilians and soldiers steadily increased, as did the number of allies throughout the Italian Peninsula. Eventually, Rome reached a point where its sheer numerical supremacy ensured victory in any war.

Most conquered cities and peoples on the Italian Peninsula retained local autonomy. When a state had been defeated, those in power were generally required to cede part of their territory to Rome. That land was then divided among Roman citizens, rich and poor alike. Sometimes, Rome established a military colony of able-bodied men to keep watch over a conquered region.

The Latins, the people most closely allied to Rome, were treated the most liberally. Latin men were even allowed to vote in the *comitia tributa* (assembly of the people) when they were in Rome. Other peoples, while they were not allowed to exercise any influence in the political sphere, nevertheless enjoyed many other privileges of Roman citizenship. Cities that had such rights were known as *municipia* (municipalities). The Romans did not think of those people as their subjects; they were termed *socii* (allies) and were considered to be sharing the interests of Rome.

into a corner. Pyrrhus returned to the Italian Peninsula to relieve the Tarentans, and in 275 BCE, his army met the Romans near Malventum. This time, his depleted forces were no match for the Romans. Pyrrhus's normally indomitable elephants were routed by a hail of burning arrows, turning the tide of battle inexorably against him. Acknowledging that his power in Italy was waning, Pyrrhus returned to Epirus. In 272 BCE, Tarentum was forced to recognize Rome's superiority.

Rome triumphant

By 270 BCE, all of the Italian Peninsula south of the Po River was subject to

See also:

Early Rome (page 6) • The Punic Wars (page 32)

THE PUNIC WARS

For much of the third century BCE, Rome was engaged in a titanic battle for control of the western Mediterranean region. Rome's adversary was the city of Carthage. The struggles came to be known as the Punic Wars.

After Rome defeated the Greek mercenary general Pyrrhus in 275 BCE, the Greek colony of Tarentum was forced to acknowledge Roman sovereignty. The victory left Rome as one of the two great powers in the western Mediterranean. The other was Carthage, on the north coast of Africa.

Carthage

Carthage was founded by Phoenician traders around the late ninth century BCE. Sited on a peninsula in the Gulf of Tunis, the city soon became a dominant player in Mediterranean trade. However, Carthage was also a military power, and by the sixth century BCE, it controlled almost the whole length of the north coast of Africa, from the Atlantic to what is now Libya, and had taken over the Balearic Islands, Malta, Sardinia, and parts of Sicily. By the fourth century BCE, Carthage had become a powerful commercial metropolis at the center of a vast web of trading posts.

Rome was naturally suspicious of its powerful neighbor, and in all the trading treaties between the two states, Rome inserted a clause that forbade Carthage from establishing any permanent bases on the Italian Peninsula. However, the Carthaginians' control of the western half of the nearby island of Sicily would prove to be the catalyst for war.

Messana

The immediate cause of the Punic Wars between Rome and Carthage was apparently insignificant. The Sicilian city of Messana, which held an important position on the narrow strait between Sicily and Italy, had fallen into the hands of a group of Italian mercenaries called the Mamertines, who had turned it into a pirates' den. Their primary victims were Sicilian Greeks. In 264 BCE, King Hiero of Syracuse laid siege to Messana in an attempt to rid the island of the renegades. In response, the Mamertines appealed to both Carthage and Rome for help. A Carthaginian fleet arrived and succeeded in getting Hiero to stand down. However, rather than allying themselves with their saviors, the Mamertines offered their allegiance to Rome. With some reluctance, the Roman senate agreed to send an expeditionary force to relieve Messana of its now unwelcome guests, thereby initiating the First Punic War, which raged for the next 23 years.

The First Punic War

The Carthaginians withdrew when the Roman force arrived, but Carthage later sent a larger army to regain Messana, enlisting Hiero's support in its struggle against Rome. However, within a year, Hiero switched sides and threw in his lot

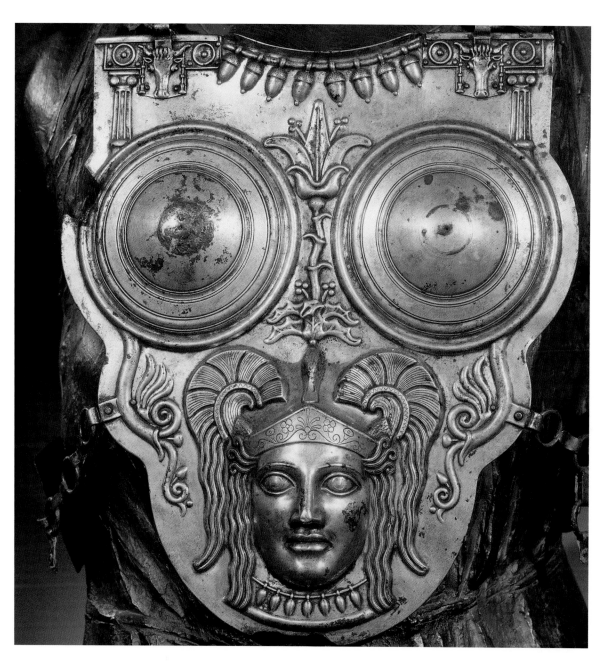

with the Romans. With Hiero as their ally, the Romans advanced across Sicily to lay siege to the Carthaginian city of Agrigentum, which they took and sacked in 262 BCE.

Despite these successes, it became clear to the Romans that they needed to break the Carthaginian's power on the seas. The Romans had little in the way of a fleet of their own, and it became imperative that they build one to match that of Carthage. According to one story, the Romans enlisted Hiero's help in designing new warships. According to another story, they used a wrecked Carthaginian galley as a model. Besides building a fleet of warships, the Romans also trained their soldiers in boarding

This brass Carthaginian breastplate dates to around the third century BCE, the period when Carthage was at war with Rome.

33

COMMERCE IN THE EARLY ROMAN EMPIRE

While the Romans were engaged in conquering Italy and parts of the Mediterranean, their interest in industry and commerce lagged far behind their military skills. During the third and second centuries BCE, craft manufacture remained in the hands of small, independent tradesmen. There was no Roman center of industry to compare with the former Etruscan city of Capua, which produced ceramics, bronzes, furniture, and perfume.

Rome imported far more than it exported. Large quantities of grain came from Sicily, and enormous amounts of silver arrived from mines in Spain. Slaves were in great demand to work on the growing landholdings of the wealthy and to service the increasingly luxurious houses of the rich in Rome and other cities. In 218 BCE, the Roman senate passed a law forbidding senators to own ships. Because of this law, most of this sea trade was carried by ships owned by Greek and Phoenician merchants.

However, while the Romans were uninterested in trade, they were to become very active in money-lending and banking. This development was a direct result of the wars of conquest, which sent a flood of gold and silver into the city.

Moneylending was a lucrative field of business. Although rates of interest were strictly controlled in Rome itself, Roman financiers could reap huge profits in the provinces by lending money to enable people to pay their taxes. Rates of interest could be extremely high, sometimes 25 percent or more. Such practices made some citizens extremely wealthy, and with the spread of wealth, a system of banking developed. A rich Roman citizen could have an account with a banker, enabling the citizen to pay large debts with paper, such as a letter of credit.

This amphitheater is located at Ostia, the ancient port of Rome. In the days of the republic, many imported goods would have passed through Ostia.

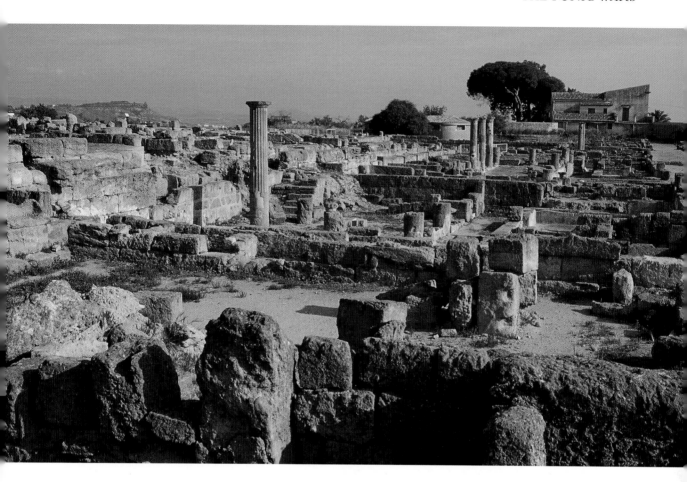

techniques. To do so, they used wooden boarding platforms with a spike at the end to hold the enemy ship in place. Such a boarding device was known as a *corvus*, the Latin word for "raven."

Early battles

In 260 BCE, the new Roman warships, numbering 140 and under the command of the consul Duilius, met the Carthaginian fleet of 130 ships at Mylae, off the northern coast of Sicily. The warships of that time had a long projecting beam, called a *rostrum* (beak), at the bow, which was used for ramming and sinking enemy ships. Ramming was the usual method of naval warfare; boarding an enemy ship was not considered important, so when the Carthaginians closed in on the Roman vessels, they were astonished to see the Romans lower boarding bridges to connect with their ships. Fully armed legionnaires then swarmed across to the enemy ships and massacred the Carthaginians in hand-to-hand combat.

Four years later, the Carthaginians were defeated in another naval battle, at Ecnomus, off the southern coast of Sicily. The Romans then decided to take an unprecedented gamble, sending an expeditionary force to Africa to attack the city of Carthage itself. The venture turned out to be a disastrous mistake. The Carthaginian infantry had been reorganized and trained by the Spartan mercenary general Xanthippus, and in the spring of 255 BCE, he engaged the Roman invaders at Bagradas in northern Africa. There, he inflicted a devastating

These ruins are located in the Sicilian town of Agrigentum. Known as Akragas at the time, the city was sacked by both the Romans and the Carthaginians during the Second Punic War.

This 16th-century-CE painting by Jacopo Ripanda depicts the Battle of Mylae. In the bottom right-hand corner, Roman soldiers can be seen boarding an enemy warship.

defeat on the Romans. The few men who survived the massacre were picked up by the Roman fleet, which was then caught in a heavy storm that sank three-quarters of the ships.

The scene of action then reverted to Sicily. In 254 BCE, the Romans captured Panormus (present-day Palermo) on the north coast of the island. However, they were later harassed by the Carthaginian general Hamilcar Barca, who arrived in Sicily in 247 BCE and established a base on Mount Eryx on the west coast. He played a game of military hide-and-seek with his opponents, conducting raids against targets both in Sicily and along the Italian coast.

By 241 BCE, both Carthage and Rome were close to exhaustion. In desperation, the Roman citizens themselves paid to outfit one final fleet. A fleet of 200 ships set sail to close off Hamilcar's Sicilian bases in Drepana and Lilybaeum. The Carthaginians sent a fleet to relieve their general and met the Roman ships at the Aegates Islands, just off the coast near Drepana. After a fierce battle, the Carthaginian fleet was destroyed. Forced to accept defeat, the Carthaginians faced punitive conditions for peace. When the ceasefire was signed, Hamilcar and the Roman consul in command in Sicily agreed that Carthage would surrender Sicily, release all prisoners, and pay a total of 2,200 gold talents to Rome over a period of 20 years.

Delegates then arrived from Rome and set even more stringent conditions. They demanded an additional 1,000 talents, half to be paid immediately and the rest over 10 years. Carthage had no option but to agree. The debt caused enormous financial distress and meant that the city could not afford to pay the mercenary troops it had used in the Sicilian campaign. When these soldiers returned to Carthage, they incited the city's Libyan slaves to rebel. Carthage called on Hamilcar to put down the insurrection, but he was unable to subdue the rebels until 238 BCE. Rome made good use of the three years of confusion by seizing the islands of Sardinia and Corsica.

Carthaginians in Spain

Carthage made Hamilcar Barca the commander-in-chief of its army in 237 BCE, and with Sicily, Sardinia, and Corsica lost to Rome, he made Spain the scene of his operations. Hamilcar spent the next nine years subjugating the Celtic tribes on the Iberian Peninsula and organizing them into an army.

When Hamilcar died in 228 BCE, his son-in-law Hasdrubal succeeded him. The new commander continued the Iberian campaign with the assistance of Hamilcar's 18-year-old son, Hannibal. Their conquests included mining regions that greatly contributed to the Carthaginian treasury. Together, these gains in material wealth and manpower

went a long way toward restoring Carthage's power. Seeing this, the Romans thought it advisable to stop this expansion in Spain before Carthage completely recovered from its defeat. Accordingly, in 226 BCE, the Romans forced Hasdrubal to sign a treaty agreeing that his troops would not cross the Ebro River in northern Spain.

Hasdrubal was killed by assassins in 221 BCE, after which the 25-year-old Hannibal assumed command of the army. In the campaigns that followed, the young general proved to have one of the greatest military minds in history.

This Roman bust of Hannibal was made from marble during the Carthaginian general's own lifetime.

37

New Roman provinces

One result of the First Punic War was that Rome now controlled territories beyond the Italian Peninsula—Corsica, Sardinia, and part of Sicily. The Romans called these territories *provincia* (provinces), and they did not consider them to be allies, but subjugated areas. Placed under the rule of Roman civil servants, the provinces suffered the same conditions as they had under the Carthaginians. Every year, two new praetors (consular deputies) were appointed, one to rule Sicily and the other to rule Sardinia and Corsica, bringing the total number of praetors to four.

After the First Punic War, the Romans used the term *mare nostrum* (meaning "our sea") for the waters around the Italian Peninsula and their new islands. As Rome's empire grew, so did the area of sea that they claimed. Eventually, the whole Mediterranean would become the *mare nostrum*.

The Second Punic War

Within two years of taking command of the Carthaginian army in Spain, Hannibal annexed all the territory between the Tagus and Ebro rivers. Hannibal had inherited a deep hatred of Rome from his father, and he was intent on rebuilding the power and wealth of Carthage, possibly with the idea of challenging Rome at some point in the future. That opportunity came when Rome interfered in the affairs of Saguntum, a city that lay south of the Ebro River and was therefore in territory that Hannibal considered to belong to Carthage. In the spring of 219 BCE, he laid siege to Saguntum, which appealed to Rome for help. The senate promised assistance, but it never arrived, and the city fell to Hannibal after eight months. Declaring Hannibal's attack to be a violation of the Ebro treaty, the Romans insisted that Hannibal be surrendered to them. When Carthage refused, the Romans declared war.

The Romans had seriously underestimated the revived strength of Carthage. During his time in Spain, Hannibal had built upon the foundations laid by his father and recruited and trained a formidable army, larger than any previously put in the field by the Carthaginians. In response to this danger, the Romans sent out two forces, one to Carthage and one to Spain to engage Hannibal. However, Hannibal had no intention of waiting for the Romans to arrive. Instead, he planned to attack them on their home ground. He assembled an army of some 40,000 troops and cavalry and, using battle-trained elephants to carry supplies,

This bust depicts the Roman general Scipio Africanus, who was largely responsible for the ultimate defeat of Carthage in the Second Punic War.

he set out from New Carthage (present-day Cartagena in southeastern Spain) and headed for Rome by land. He crossed the Pyrenees Mountains and the Rhone River and marched east along the Mediterranean coast.

Hannibal in Italy

To reach the Italian Peninsula, Hannibal's army had to cross the Alps, a feat that has become one of the most famous in military history. The march took 15 days. The Carthaginians had to contend with snowstorms and avalanches, as well as attacks from mountain tribes. Most of the elephants and some 15,000 men died from cold or starvation. However, by the fall of 218 BCE, Hannibal and his army had reached the Po Valley, around 80 miles (129 km) south of the Alps, and were prepared to take on the forces Rome was assembling.

The first Roman general to confront Hannibal was the consul Publius Cornelius Scipio. Scipio had initially been dispatched to Spain, but he hastily returned when news of Hannibal's invasion reached him. The two generals met at the Ticinus River. Even though they were considerably depleted, Hannibal's forces had no difficulty in defeating the Romans. Scipio retreated to the base of the Apennine Mountains, where he awaited the arrival of another Roman force, under Sempronius Longus, which had originally been assembled for an attack on Carthage. The combined army attacked Hannibal at the Trebia River, but the Romans were encircled by the Carthaginians and lost two-thirds of their men. After this disastrous Roman defeat, the road to the south was open for Hannibal.

Defeat at Trasimene

In the spring of 217 BCE, the Roman senate dispatched one consul with an army to Ariminum on the Adriatic coast,

Hannibal's greatest victory over the Romans came at the Battle of Cannae. This illustration of the battle comes from a 15th-century-CE manuscript.

while the other, Gaius Flaminius, was posted at Arretium in Etruria. As soon as he received news that Hannibal was on the move in Etruria, Flaminius followed with his army. Anxious to catch up with the Carthaginians, Flaminius made forced marches and neglected to send out scouts to reconnoiter the surrounding terrain. He was caught in a narrow pass near Lake Trasimene, where Hannibal's forces suddenly surrounded Flaminius's army and wiped it out.

In Rome, a nervous crowd waited for news. At dusk, the praetor Marcus Pomponius appeared before the senate building. Without preamble, he simply said: "A great battle was fought and we were completely defeated." Although all

Rome was in shock, there was no panic. Instead, the famous patrician Quintus Fabius Maximus Verrucosus was appointed dictator—the special office held only in time of dire emergency.

Contrary to expectations after the defeat at Lake Trasimene, Hannibal did not march on Rome. Instead, he passed on to southern Italy, where he unsuccessfully attempted to persuade the southern cities to defect and ally themselves with him. Hannibal was pursued by a Roman army led by the newly appointed dictator, Fabius, who avoided any direct confrontation. This policy was unpopular in Rome and soon earned Fabius the nickname *cunctator* (dawdler). Nevertheless, Fabius eventually inflicted some serious damage on Hannibal, and his presence encouraged the southern Italian cities to remain loyal to Rome.

The Battle of Cannae

Hannibal spent the winter of 217–216 BCE at Gerontium, moving his army to Cannae on the Ofanto River in the spring. When Fabius's six-month term as dictator was over, command of the Roman army was given to two new consuls, Gaius Terentius Varro and Lucius Aemilius Paulus. In the summer, they led their army of around 85,000 men toward Hannibal's encampment at Cannae. Hannibal, with his smaller army of 55,000, prepared to fight on the plain before the city.

The engagement that followed was a classic example of Hannibal's military genius. Hannibal arranged his infantry in a convex shape, with his weakest troops at the very center. When the Romans made a frontal attack, the center fell back to lead the enemy into a trap. Hannibal's veteran infantry, positioned on the flanks, advanced and turned inward to trap the Romans. At this point, Hannibal's cavalry, having defeated its Roman counterpart, wheeled around from the rear to cut off any Roman retreat. The encircled Roman army was largely destroyed; it was the most disastrous defeat Rome had ever suffered. Some 50,000 Roman and allied soldiers died, including the consul Aemilius Paulus. Varro escaped with what was left of the army. Hannibal lost only 6,000 men.

The Magnanimity of Scipio Africanus *by Bernardino Fungai depicts the Roman general as a Renaissance prince. The painting dates to around the beginning of the 16th century CE.*

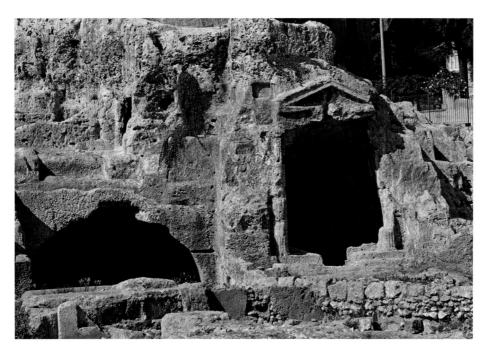

The tomb of Archimedes is found in Syracuse, Sicily. The Greek inventor's war machines helped defend the city against Roman attack.

Even after this catastrophe, Rome would not capitulate, refusing even to receive Hannibal's messengers. The prognosis was dire, however. In addition to Rome's unprecedented loss of men, another problem for the Romans was that the southern cities were now defecting to Hannibal. Rome raised new legions and prepared for further resistance. However, Hannibal himself was in need of reinforcements, which Carthage failed to send. Instead of marching on Rome, he tried, and failed, to take Naples. He then retired to Capua, Italy's second largest city, which opened its gates to him. Hannibal wintered there, while more cities defected to him.

Fighting on three fronts

After the Battle of Cannae, the Romans adopted the skirmishing tactics that had previously been used by Fabius, limiting themselves to small battles and expeditions to punish deserting allies. They still ruled the sea, and this dominance made it difficult for Carthage to send reinforcements to Hannibal.

The war continued on three fronts. On the Italian Peninsula, deserting allies were gradually resubjugated by the Romans. In 212 BCE, Hannibal won the important seaboard city of Tarentum, but the following year, he lost Capua, which the Romans starved into submission. This loss cost Hannibal the support of many of his other Italian allies.

On Sicily, Syracuse had been an ally of Rome under King Hiero, but after he died in 215 BCE, Syracuse sided with Carthage. A Roman expeditionary force laid siege to Syracuse in 213 BCE but was temporarily rebuffed, partly by the ingenious war machines invented by the Greek mathematician Archimedes, a citizen of Syracuse. The city finally fell to the Romans in 212 BCE through treachery, and in the ensuing looting by Roman soldiers, Archimedes was killed.

On the third front, in Spain, the Carthaginian army was now commanded by Hannibal's brother Hasdrubal (not to be confused with his brother-in-law of the same name). A Roman expeditionary force under the brothers Publius

41

Cornelius and Gnaeus Cornelius Scipio harassed Hasdrubal and gained the allegiance of tribes north of the Ebro River. In 211 BCE, the brothers crossed the Ebro and took Saguntum. However, they were compelled to divide their dwindling forces. As a result, the Romans were defeated in two separate battles, and both Scipios were killed.

Carthage loses Spain

In 210 BCE, Rome sent another army to Spain, this time commanded by the son and namesake of Publius Cornelius Scipio. This 25-year-old, later to be known as Scipio Africanus, had served in northern Italy against Hannibal and had held the office of *aedile* (magistrate), even though theoretically he had been too young to do so. He was granted his command by the *comitia centuriata* (military assembly), which also bestowed on him the rank of proconsul. This honor gave him the same authority as a consul. The assembly's confidence in the young Scipio was not misplaced; he was to prove himself one of the greatest generals of the ancient world.

After landing in Spain, Scipio quickly restored the morale of the defeated troops, leading them to one victory after another. In 209 BCE, he led a surprise attack and took New Carthage, where Hasdrubal had his headquarters, arsenals, and main base of supplies. The following year, Scipio defeated Hasdrubal at the Battle of Baecula, but the Carthaginian managed to retreat with most of his army intact. Hasdrubal decided to abandon Spain and try to reach his brother Hannibal in Italy. Scipio allowed him to leave, rather than risk a dangerous pursuit through the Alps.

A new Carthaginian army was then assembled in Spain, and in 206 BCE, this new force faced Scipio and his army at the Battle of Ilipa near Seville. Thanks to the tactical brilliance of Scipio, the Carthaginian forces were enveloped and utterly destroyed. By the end of the year, Carthage had surrendered Spain to Rome for good.

Hasdrubal crosses the Alps

Hasdrubal succeeded in marching overland to Italy and, in 207 BCE, crossed the Alps to reach the northern Italian Peninsula. Augmenting his army with troops supplied by Gauls and Ligurians, he proceeded south, intending to meet up with Hannibal and mount a joint attack on Rome. However, he was surprised at the Metaurus River by a Roman force under the command of the consul Gaius Claudius Nero. In the ensuing battle, Hasdrubal's army was annihilated, and he himself was killed. The Romans announced Hasdrubal's defeat by beheading him and tossing his head into his brother Hannibal's camp.

War in Africa

Scipio returned to Rome in 205 BCE and was elected consul. He then persuaded the senate to allow him to take the war to Africa and punish the Carthaginians on their home ground. First, he took his army to Sicily and spent a year training it in the battle tactics (based on Hannibal's own methods) that had won him success at the battles of Baecula and Ilipa. Then, in 204 BCE, he landed on African soil, where he was met with fierce resistance. However, in the spring, he made a surprise night attack on the enemy's camps, setting fire to them and putting the troops to the sword. The Carthaginians reassembled their forces, only to be completely destroyed by Scipio at the Battle of the Great Plains that same summer.

In a last-ditch attempt to retrieve the situation, Hannibal was recalled from Italy. In 202 BCE, Hannibal visited Scipio in his tent to discuss a number of peace proposals. Scipio would not accept

This undated modern painting depicts Scipio's victory procession after the Battle of Zama in 202 BCE.

them, and Hannibal decided to risk everything in a final battle. The two sides met in October at the Battle of Zama. Hannibal's new recruits fled, and his veterans were cut down by the cavalry of the Romans' African ally, Masinissa. The Carthaginian army was almost totally destroyed, but Hannibal was one of the few survivors. Scipio's victory at Zama brought the Second Punic War to an end and earned him the title Africanus the Elder.

The death of Hannibal

Under the peace treaty signed between Carthage and Rome in 201 BCE, Carthage was required to yield Spain to Rome, dismantle its fleet, and pay the sum of 10,000 gold talents over 50 years. Carthage was forbidden to wage war outside Africa, and only with Rome's permission within Africa.

Hannibal returned to Carthage, where he took up a political role, amending the constitution and reforming its government and financial system. He became unpopular with some aristocrats, who accused him of plotting with Antioch III of Syria to make war on Rome. Fearful of Rome's retribution, Hannibal fled to Antioch's court at Ephesus in 195 BCE and advised the king on war with Rome.

When Antioch was defeated at Magnesia in 190 BCE, Rome demanded that he surrender Hannibal. Fearing for his life, Hannibal fled once more, eventually taking refuge with Prusias II, king of Bithynia in Anatolia. The king could barely control the pirates on his shores, much less protect Hannibal from the Romans, who again demanded his surrender. Around 183 BCE, rather than fall into Roman hands, Hannibal took poison and ended his own life.

See also:

Rome's Early Wars and Conquests (page 24)

REVOLUTION AND REFORM

TIME LINE

197 BCE

Roman victory at Battle of Cynoscephalae ends Second Macedonian War.

146 BCE

Carthage falls to Roman force under Scipio Aemilianus.

133 BCE

Tiberius Gracchus elected tribune; murdered later that year.

123 BCE

Gaius Gracchus elected tribune; uses office to force social change.

108 BCE

Gaius Marius elected consul; goes on to hold office further six times.

88 BCE

Lucius Cornelius Sulla marches on Rome at head of army and drives opponents from city.

82 BCE

Sulla declares himself dictator.

In the second and early first centuries BCE, Rome continued to gain new territory. At the same time, there was social upheaval at home. Class conflict eventually led to one aristocrat, Lucius Cornelius Sulla, marching on Rome at the head of an army.

Rome's victory over Carthage in 201 BCE made Rome the preeminent power in the western Mediterranean region. However, although the Italian Peninsula had suffered greatly during the course of the Second Punic War, Rome continued with its military exploits. The ruling elite wanted to punish the Macedonian king, Philip V, for his alliance with the Carthaginian general Hannibal. In 200 BCE, in response to requests for help from Pergamum and Rhodes, a Roman army was sent into Greece. The expedition marked the start of the short-lived Second Macedonian War (see box, page 46). The war came to an end in 197 BCE, when the Romans inflicted a decisive defeat on Philip at the Battle of Cynoscephalae. This victory ensured that Rome dominated the eastern Mediterranean region as well as the western.

Roman armies moved swiftly from one conflict to another. They next marched against Antioch III, the king of Syria, defeating him at the Battle of Magnesia in 190 BCE. The once great Seleucid Empire was forced into an ignominious peace, ceding all its holdings in Anatolia and Europe to Rome.

The *latifundia*

While these developments were happening abroad, a social revolution was taking place at home. Much of the land that had been seized during the Punic Wars fell into the hands of the wealthy in the form of vast land holdings called *latifundia* (large estates). These estates were run either as mixed farms producing grain, wine, and olives, or as ranch-type operations supporting large herds of sheep and cattle. Both types were generally worked by slaves rather than free men, an arrangement that had several advantages from the owners' point of view. Slaves worked long hours, could not be called away to do military service, and did not have to be paid wages. These large estates squeezed out the small peasant farmers, many of whom sold out to the large landowners and then either hired themselves out as day laborers, if they could find work, or migrated to Rome for employment there.

Corruption in this new society was rife, particularly in the field of tax collection. Civil servants in the provinces sold regional concessions for tax collection at high prices. Wealthy noblemen then formed large consortiums to purchase such concessions. They then leased out their licenses to *publicani* (tax collectors), who paid up front and then recouped

This mosaic from the second century CE depicts horses being used to thresh wheat. Large estates such as that depicted here were known as **latifundia.**

THE MACEDONIAN WARS

During the Second Punic War, Hannibal formed an alliance with King Philip V of Macedon. The move incensed the Romans, who dispatched a fleet under the general Valerius Laevinus to the Adriatic in 214 BCE. Over the course of the next nine years, there were a number of skirmishes between Roman and Macedonian forces, but no large-scale, conclusive battles. In 205 BCE, the Romans made peace with Philip. This largely uneventful struggle is known as the First Macedonian War.

After the Second Punic War ended in 201 BCE, the senate felt that not enough had been done to punish Philip for his alliance with Hannibal. The senate was also alarmed by the fact that Philip was seeking to extend his influence in the Aegean and had attacked several Greek city-states in the area. In 200 BCE, a Roman force of around 30,000 men was sent to Apollonia in Illyria, north of Macedon. In 197 BCE, the Romans confronted Philip's forces at the Battle of Cynoscephalae. Philip was defeated, and under the terms of the peace treaty, he was forced to give up all of his possessions outside of Macedon and pay a massive sum of money to Rome. As a result of this treaty, Rome now dominated almost the entire Mediterranean region.

The Third Macedonian War broke out when Perseus, the ambitious son and successor of Philip V, incensed the Roman senate by entering into treaties with neighboring city-states. In 171 BCE, Rome declared war on Perseus, and initially, Perseus achieved some successes in his engagements with the Roman army. However, in 168 BCE, he suffered an ignominious defeat at the Battle of Pydna. As at Cynoscephalae, the Macedonian army, using its traditional phalanx formation, proved to be no match for the Roman troops with their more flexible tactics. Perseus was taken prisoner and escorted in chains back to Rome, where he was sentenced to life imprisonment. His country was divided into four republics, all of which had to pay annual tribute to their Roman conquerors.

In 152 BCE, a pretender to the throne of Macedonia, called Andriscus, attempted to restore the monarchy and unite the four republics in an alliance against Rome. A Roman army under Quintus Caecilius Metellus was sent to put down the rebellion and had no difficulty in expelling the pretender. As a result, Macedonia was finally made a province of Rome in 148 BCE.

This sculpture from the first century CE depicts Philip V of Macedon, a former ally of the Carthaginian general Hannibal.

their outlay by collecting the taxes. Everyone but the tax payer made a significant profit.

Attempts at reform

Many people spoke out against the corruption, demanding a return to the Roman tradition of integrity. The most famous voice belonged to Marcus Porcius Cato (234–149 BCE), also known as Cato the Elder. Cato was a prosperous gentleman farmer who had once been awarded a triumph for his military service in Spain. He had also served as quaestor (junior magistrate) in 204 BCE, as aedile (temple functionary) in 199 BCE, as praetor (consular deputy) in 198 BCE, and as consul in 195 BCE. When serving as censor in 184 BCE, he suspended any senator he considered to be immoral or unworthy of office. Opposed to Greek influence on Rome, Cato believed that most of the city's problems could be solved by a return to ancient Roman traditions.

In 157 BCE, Cato was sent to Africa to mediate in a conflict between the Carthaginians and the Numidians. He came back convinced that Carthage was an even worse threat to Rome than Greece. Until his death in 149 BCE, he closed every speech with the words *delenda est Carthago* (meaning "Carthage must be destroyed"). His considerable influence helped to bring about the Third Punic War (see box, page 49), which achieved just that aim.

Other agitation for reform came from a group of senators who were political enemies of Cato. This faction was led by Tiberius Sempronius Gracchus (168–133 BCE). Tiberius Gracchus had a distinguished military record. He fought in the Third Punic War and was said to have been the first Roman soldier to scale the wall of Carthage in the battle that destroyed the city in 146 BCE. During the Spanish Wars of 154 to 133

BCE, when the native tribes sought to free themselves from Roman oppression, Tiberius served as quaestor to the Roman army in Spain. In 137 BCE, he saved 20,000 defeated Roman troops from slaughter by negotiating with the victorious city of Numantia.

On his return to Rome, Tiberius saw that Roman society was polarized between a small group of very rich aristocrats, many of whom were corrupt, and a mass of landless peasants. Much public land had been illegally appropriated by large landowners after the Second Punic War, leaving many rural areas more or less depopulated of peasants. These areas could only be repopulated by offering the peasants land, which would entail recovering and redistributing land that had formerly been public property. With this program in mind, Tiberius presented himself as a candidate for the post of tribune of the people.

Tiberius was elected in 133 BCE and immediately presented a land reform bill

In this 18th-century-CE illustration, the tribune Gaius Gracchus addresses the popular assembly.

This relief sculpture depicts a Roman shopkeeper.

directly to the *concilium plebis*, by-passing the senate. The aristocratic senators, led by Tiberius's cousin Scipio Africanus the Younger, not only saw this as a threat to their landholdings, but also to their political power—normally, such bills were discussed by the senate before they were presented to the *concilium plebis*. The senators persuaded another tribune, Marcus Octavius, to veto the bill. Not deterred by this, Tiberius convinced the assembly to remove the troublesome tribune from office. This action was unprecedented, but Tiberius defended it by arguing that it was as

necessary as the driving out of kings—the interests of the people took precedence over the immunity of the tribune. After this initial setback, the assembly voted through the land reform bill without further difficulty.

A commission set up to implement the reform consisted of Tiberius, his brother Gaius, and his father-in-law Appius Claudius Pulcher. However, their work was sabotaged at every step by the senate. Tiberius proposed using funds from the recently acquired province of Asia to help the newly settled peasants buy stock. However, this idea enraged

THE THIRD PUNIC WAR

Although the wealth and power of Carthage were badly damaged by the Second Punic War, which ended in 201 BCE, the city gradually began to regain its status in the half-century that followed. However, it suffered constant harassment from its neighbor, Numidia, which made a series of incursions into Carthaginian territory. When Carthage took steps to raise an army to defend its borders (in direct breach of its peace treaty with Rome), the senate acted swiftly. It dispatched a large combined land and sea force, under both consuls, to deal with Carthage once and for all. The city was besieged, but it proved difficult to take. One of the new consuls elected in 147 BCE was Scipio Aemilianus, the adopted grandson of Scipio Africanus the Elder, who had defeated Carthage at Zama in 202 BCE. The young Scipio was given the task of bringing Carthage to its knees.

In 146 BCE, Scipio managed to breach the outer wall of the city. The Carthaginian garrison, although weakened by hunger, put up strong resistance, and it took a week of hand-to-hand fighting through the streets to reach the citadel, where the remaining 50,000 citizens were huddled. Scipio took them all prisoner (later selling them into slavery) and set fire to the buildings, letting them burn to the ground. He cursed the ruins, pouring salt on them, and forbade reoccupation of the site for 25 years. The territory of Carthage became the new Roman province of Africa.

the senate, which considered the government of the provinces to be its own prerogative. When his term of office expired, Tiberius stood for reelection, anxious to see through his reforms. This act was another unprecedented move, and for Tiberius, it proved a step too far. In the heated arguments that followed his announcement, several senators, together with their armed slaves and clients, surrounded Tiberius and beat him to death. His body was thrown into the Tiber River. Some 300 of Tiberius's followers met a similar fate.

Following Tiberius's death in 133 BCE, the Roman senate divided into two factions. The progressive *populares* (advocates of the people) wanted to continue the reforms of Tiberius, while the *optimates* (aristocrats) wanted the senate to retain all power. The land reform law was left in place, but little was done to implement it.

Gaius Sempronius Gracchus

Tiberius's younger brother Gaius Gracchus (c. 153–121 BCE) was an even more fervent reformer than Tiberius. He was elected tribune of the people in 123 BCE. His many proposals had one objective, that of weakening the power of the *optimates*. Gaius first attacked the jury system under which provincial governors were tried on charges of corruption. These juries usually consisted of senators. Gaius introduced a bill that gave this responsibility to the *equites*, members of the business class.

Gaius then turned his attention to the poor of Rome. He established the *lex frumentaria* (grain law), which provided for the distribution of grain to the citizens at a fixed price, subsidized by the state. He also pursued an active policy to relocate the rootless people of Rome's streets to new colonies, including one amid the ruins of Carthage. In contrast to his brother, Gaius was reelected tribune without difficulty in 122 BCE.

During his second term of office, Gaius introduced a bill that would grant full civil rights to the Italian allies. This move was not popular with his fellow Romans, however. The bill was defeated, and Gaius was not elected for a third term. The senate then canceled the colonization of Carthage, claiming that the city was eternally cursed.

Without the protection of office, Gaius was vulnerable to attack. In a riot that followed a demonstration organized by Gaius, a servant of one of the consuls was killed. The death gave the *optimates* a pretext to have the senate declare a state of emergency. The consul Lucius Opimius assembled a vigilante patrol that attacked Gaius and his guards on the Aventine Hill, where they had taken refuge. Determined not to fall into the hands of his enemies, Gaius ordered his own slave to stab him to death. Some 3,000 of Gaius's followers were subsequently indicted and executed.

For the moment, the senate had triumphed, but it was a hollow victory. Rome desperately needed a new constitution. While the old form of government had been adequate for running a city, it was hopelessly unsuitable now that Rome had become a regional power.

Expanding the empire

While attempts at reform were taking place at home, Rome's armies were continuing to gain territory abroad. After annexing Macedonia, Rome acquired territory in Anatolia. In 133 BCE, the king of Pergamum died and left his kingdom to Rome in his will. The region became the province of Asia.

After driving the Carthaginians out of Spain in 206 BCE, the Romans had divided the Iberian Peninsula into two provinces. However, mismanagement by the provincial governors led to years of rebellion. Not surprisingly, governmental service in Spain was not popular among Roman citizens. One of the centers of resistance to Rome was the small northern city of Numantia, the chief stronghold of the Celtiberians (Celts living on the Iberian Peninsula). Numantia held out against the Romans for nine years. Eventually, the Roman general Scipio Aemilianus successfully blockaded the city, which was then driven by hunger to surrender in 133 BCE. Scipio destroyed the city and sold the survivors into slavery.

This 19th-century-CE lithograph depicts the Roman general Scipio Aemilianus watching the destruction of Carthage.

Trouble in Africa

Toward the end of the second century BCE, Rome became involved in a civil war in Numidia, a kingdom in northern Africa (part of present-day Algeria). During the course of the struggle, a number of Italian merchants were massacred by troops belonging to Jugurtha, one of the rival claimants to the throne. In 111 BCE, a Roman army was sent to Numidia to punish Jugurtha. However, the campaign dragged on for two years.

In 109 BCE, the consul Caecilius Metellus was put in charge of the army in Africa. He restored order and discipline among the troops and began a campaign to defeat and capture Jugurtha. However, Jugurtha's greater knowledge of the local terrain allowed him to stay out of Roman hands.

Metellus had a capable deputy in Gaius Marius (157–86 BCE), an *eques* who had risen to the position of senator. Marius was ambitious and begged leave of his commanding officer in order to return to Rome and seek election as consul. He was successful in obtaining the office in 108 BCE. The *comitia tributa* (assembly of the people) then appointed him commander-in-chief in Africa— an appointment hitherto made only by the senate.

Marius returned to Africa with a levy of raw recruits, which he proceeded to train to a high standard. He continued the war against Jugurtha, capturing the treasury and inflicting considerable losses on Jugurtha's forces. However, Marius still could not capture Jugurtha.

Eventually, the questor Lucius Cornelius Sulla (138–78 BCE) entered into negotiations with Bocchus I, king of Mauretania, who was Jugurtha's father-in-law. In 106 BCE, Bocchus was persuaded to hand the Numidian king over to the Roman army. This act ended the war; Jugurtha was taken to Rome, where he was executed.

This bust depicts the Roman general and statesman Gaius Marius, who is best known for the reforms he made to the Roman army.

Threat from the north

In 105 BCE, Rome came under the threat of two Germanic tribes, the Cimbrians and Teutons, who were on the move in Gaul, threatening the borders of Italy. A consular army sent to stop them was completely destroyed. It was feared that the tribes were heading for Rome. Then, to everyone's surprise, the tribes changed tack and marched toward Spain, giving Rome a respite.

In 104 BCE, the people elected Marius consul for a second time, hoping he would save them from the marauding northerners. He immediately formed a new army and marched into southern Gaul. In 102 BCE, Marius encountered

THE NEW ROMAN ARMY

For his campaigns in Numidia and the north, Gaius Marius raised an army from a class that had not previously been eligible for military service. The property qualification was abolished, enabling members of the proletariat to volunteer for service, which they did in large numbers. For the poorer class of citizen, army service offered many attractions. There was a regular pay packet (although the cost of equipment was deducted from it), and on demobilization, the soldier was promised a parcel of land.

Marius subjected his new recruits to rigorous training, but however hard he drove them, his down-to-earth approach ensured that he retained his popularity. Every soldier was equipped with a sword and a javelin and was drilled to become highly proficient in single hand-to-hand combat. Marius made the troops carry their own heavy equipment, so they were not dependent on a baggage train, and raised their power of endurance by setting them arduous tasks such as digging canals.

Many of Marius's recruits became professional soldiers, which changed the character of the army from that of a temporary militia assembled for a specific campaign to that of a regular standing army. Soldiers now had great feelings of loyalty to their comrades-in-arms, to their legion, and to their commanding officer. One effect of this change was that since the soldiers' strongest bond of loyalty was to their commander, he had the potential to use them against the state.

This detail from the victory column of Marcus Aurelius depicts Roman soldiers. Marius's changes had long-term implications for the Roman army.

the Teutons at Aquae Sextiae, where he encircled and totally destroyed them. The following year, he defeated the Cimbrians at Vercellae on the northern Italian Peninsula, thereby putting an end to the threat from the north.

The social war

Once back in Rome, Marius threw himself into domestic politics, associating himself with the people's party. Its leaders had become increasingly radical, and in 100 BCE, Marius, as consul, was forced to suppress riots, which considerably dented his popularity.

The Italian cities, meanwhile, were agitating to be granted full Roman citizenship. Their contribution of men to the Roman army in recent conflicts had been considerable, and they were no longer willing to be considered subordinate allies. In 91 BCE, their cause was taken up by the tribune Marcus Livius Drusus. However, the position was so unpopular in Rome that it resulted in his assassination. When the Italian allies heard the news, they rose in revolt.

The Italian rebels formed a confederacy, founded their own capital at Corfinium (which they renamed Italia), and created a senate and magistrates like those in Rome. The rebels also raised an army, which, because many of its soldiers had been trained by Marius, was more

The tombs of the kings of the ancient region of Pontus are located in this mountainside in northeastern Turkey. The actions of one king of Pontus, Mithridates VI, led to war with Rome.

This bust, made around 50 BCE, depicts the Roman dictator Lucius Cornelius Sulla.

armies entered the province of Asia, where they were received as liberators by the populace, who had been exploited financially for almost 40 years. With the encouragement of Mithridates, the people of Asia turned on their oppressors and massacred some 80,000 Italian residents.

In Rome, the senate gave Sulla command of the forces preparing to go east to confront Mithridates, even though Marius had been hoping for the appointment. Marius was not popular with the senate, but he had plenty of support from the *equites* and the popular party, including the tribune Publius Sulpicius. Sulpicius persuaded the popular assembly to reverse the senate's decision and invest Marius with Sulla's command in Asia. The result was civil war.

Marching on Rome

In 88 BCE, Sulla journeyed to southern Italy and met up with the legions that were preparing for the campaign in Asia. In spite of the assembly's decision, the legions accepted Sulla as their leader. Sulla then took several of the legions and marched on Rome, an unprecedented step. He occupied the city and drove out Marius and many of Marius's supporters. The senate was once more firmly in control, and Sulla was confirmed in his command. He immediately departed for Pontus in the east.

Not long after Sulla left for Pontus, members of the people's party raised a new army in Etruria. Led by Marius and the consul Cinna, this army took Rome. Marius was reelected consul. The occupation rapidly degenerated into a bloodbath; many members of the aristocracy were murdered by Marius's troops. Eventually, some semblance of order and justice was restored by Cinna. Marius, beginning to show signs of madness, died early in 86 BCE. Cinna became a virtual dictator.

than a match for the Roman army. After two years of fighting, the Romans finally ended the rebellion by granting full civil rights to the citizens of every city that surrendered.

Sulla and civil war

Lucius Cornelius Sulla had distinguished himself by his leadership in the social war and was rewarded with the consulship in 88 BCE. That same year, Mithridates VI, the ambitious king of Pontus in the east, came into conflict with Rome. His

Even though he had been outlawed by his political opponents back home, Sulla continued the war against Mithridates in the east. After much hard fighting, Mithridates was forced to capitulate, and Sulla was free to confront his opponents in Rome.

Sulla triumphant

In 83 BCE, Sulla landed in Brindisium and marched once again on Rome. His forces were augmented by disaffected aristocrats who flocked to his standard. In 82 BCE, after a year of heavy fighting, Sulla occupied Rome, appointing himself dictator. A reign of terror followed. Sulla instituted a purge of his political opponents, condemning them to death or banishment. He also published proscription lists; anyone whose name appeared on them lost all his possessions and could be killed at any time.

Sulla then reorganized the government. He reformed the constitution, attempting to restore the traditional power of the senate and aristocracy, of which he himself was a member. For example, he decreed that tribunes should no longer be allowed to introduce bills to the assembly or to serve in other political positions after their term of office had finished.

When he had sufficiently strengthened the power of his class, Sulla withdrew from the political stage. In 79 BCE, he resigned his dictatorship and retired to an estate in Campania. He died the following year. However, the attempts at social change that had begun with the Gracchi brothers and continued with Marius were not yet over.

See also:

The End of the Republic (page 56)

The Temple of Hercules Victor was built in the Forum Boarium, Rome, around 120 BCE.

THE END OF THE REPUBLIC

In the late first century BCE, the Roman republic was torn apart by a series of civil wars. A number of ambitious men fought for power. The ascent of one of them—Julius Caesar—ushered in a new era of Roman history.

The first century BCE was to see the end of the Roman republic. First Pompey (106–48 BCE) and then Julius Caesar (100–44 BCE) gathered authority in their own hands as power gradually passed from the senate and the Roman people to an absolute ruler. Noted for their military as well as their political ability, Pompey and Caesar brought the whole of the Mediterranean region under Roman rule.

The aftermath of Sulla's reign

In the early first century BCE, the Roman political system had been transformed by the actions of Lucius Cornelius Sulla, who had marched on Rome and set himself up as dictator. Once he had gained power, Sulla had set about strengthening the role of the aristocrats and the senate and weakening that of both the *equites* (the business class) and the common people.

Sulla died in retirement in 78 BCE, leaving Rome to recover from 10 years of civil war and atrocities. Most Roman citizens wanted peace and a time for recovery, but Rome was threatened on several fronts. The most serious challenge came from the general and politician Quintus Sertorius. Sertorius had refused to join Sulla's invasion of Italy in 82 BCE, making instead for Spain. Claiming that he was a representative of the government in Rome, Sertorius set up a "counter senate" of prominent Roman citizens. An honest and fair administrator, he won local support across the Iberian Peninsula. Three Roman armies were sent out to unseat him, but, with the help of a locally recruited army, Sertorius was able to defeat them in quick succession.

In late 77 BCE, the senate sent a large army out to Spain to bring down Sertorius once and for all. The army's commander was 29-year-old Gnaeus Pompeius, better known as Pompey, who had been an ally of Sulla during the civil war. Pompey set out with plenty of youthful optimism, confident that he would soon accomplish his task, especially because there was already a Roman army in Spain under the command of the general Metellus Pius. However, much to his embarrassment, it took Pompey five years to achieve the senate's aim. Only when Sertorius was assassinated by his own men in 72 BCE was Pompey able to bring the war to a successful conclusion.

The military might of Rome was being stretched over several theaters of war. In 75 BCE, another major war had begun in Bithynia in Anatolia, where King Mithridates VI of Pontus had again challenged the power of Rome. Mithridates had already waged war against Rome twice and now rose up again. The senate responded by sending the consul Lucius Lucullus to command the Roman forces in that war. In the Mediterranean, meanwhile, pirates were preying on merchant ships, making trade hazardous if not impossible. The praetor Marcus Antonius (the father of the man known as Mark Antony) was given command of a naval force with a mission to rid the seas of piracy.

Spartacus

With the Roman army engaged on multiple fronts, an unprecedented event in Italy took on major importance. A group of gladiators at the Capua barracks, led by a slave named Spartacus, escaped and incited other slaves to join the rebellion. Thousands of renegade slaves formed an army so powerful that it was able to go on a rampage throughout Italy for two

This 19th-century-CE painting by Karl von Piloty depicts the murder of Julius Caesar in the senate.

57

This sculpture of the head of Pompey the Great was made during the general's lifetime.

were elected. The pair then repealed much of the legislation introduced by Sulla. The senate monopoly on the courts was abolished; in future, criminal juries were to consist of both senators and wealthy nonsenators. The power of the tribunes and censors was restored, and two elected censors at last made good the promise to grant Roman citizenship to the Italian population. Both censors were supporters of Pompey, and the move greatly enhanced Pompey's popularity.

At the end of his term of office in 69 BCE, Pompey refused to take the governorship of a province, which would have been the normal practice. Massive piracy continued to paralyze trade in the Mediterranean, and so little grain was reaching Rome that the population was threatened with starvation. In 67 BCE, Pompey was given a special command to deal with the situation. Taking over from Marcus Antonius, Pompey assumed command of a fleet of 500 ships and swept the pirates northeast to Cilicia in just 89 days. There, he offered them a choice—either give up piracy or fight to the death. Those who opted for civilian life were allowed to colonize abandoned cities along the coast.

His pursuit of the pirates brought Pompey into the vicinity of Lucullus, who had succeeded in driving Mithridates into Armenia. However, far from being a popular general, Lucullus had alienated both his own troops and Roman merchants with his rigorous enforcement of discipline and honest trading practices. Lucullus was also out of favor in Rome, and in 66 BCE, he was forced to cede his authority to Pompey. Pompey now had supreme command in the east, and he promptly put it to use by defeating Mithridates, taking his capital, and slaughtering most of his army. Mithridates himself escaped but later took his own life.

years, beating off the armies of two consuls. The rebellion was eventually halted by an army of some 40,000 men commanded by Marcus Licinius Crassus. Spartacus and his troops were finally defeated at a battle in Lucania in 71 BCE. Spartacus died in the fighting, and 6,000 of the rebel slaves were crucified along the road that led from Capua to Rome.

Pompey and Crassus

In 70 BCE, the rivals Crassus and Pompey both returned to Rome as conquering heroes, and both demanded to be made consul. In the event, Crassus and Pompey agreed to act together, and both

EXTENT OF ROMAN TERRITORY AT END OF RULE OF CAESAR

KEY

Roman territory in 44 BCE

✗ Major battle

Pompey spent the next few years consolidating Rome's position in the east. Several new provinces were created, including Syria and Cilicia. Beyond them, a string of client states protected the eastern frontiers of the empire. In 63 BCE, the independent Jewish state surrounding the city of Jerusalem was conquered and transformed into a vassal state under a client king. As victor, Pompey treated the Jews with sensitivity. It is said that when he entered the great temple in Jerusalem, he penetrated only as far as the Jewish high priests would go, although he did peer through a curtain to see the "Holy of Holies." In 62 BCE, his

tasks accomplished, Pompey returned to Rome in glory.

The influence of Cicero

Back in Rome, Pompey faced a new and powerful rival—Marcus Tullius Cicero (106–43 BCE). Cicero, a brilliant lawyer and orator, had risen to fame in 70 BCE when he won the case against Verres, the corrupt governor of Sicily. Verres had ruled in so exploitative a manner that his subjects had filed a complaint against him with the senate. Verres stood trial confident in the belief that any jury established under Sulla could be bribed and that his class and his wealth would ensure his acquittal. Times had changed, however, and much of Sulla's legislation had been repealed and criminal justice had been restored. Cicero, playing to the anti-Sullan political mood of the day, presented overwhelming evidence against Verres in an eloquent speech. Despite the mainly senatorial constitution of the court, Verres was convicted. However, corruption was still rife, both in Rome and in the provinces.

By 63 BCE, the year Cicero was made consul, the situation was ripe for revolution. On assuming office, Cicero saw that the foundation of the Roman republic was so shaky that it could be destroyed by the actions of a single commander with a strong private army. All over the Italian Peninsula, debt and discontent were rampant, and families dispossessed by Sulla wanted restitution.

In the autumn of 63 BCE, a conspiracy to overturn the government in Rome was hatched by Lucius Sergius Catilina, also known as Catiline, who had failed to bribe his way into a consulship. Cicero denounced the plot before the senate and demanded the death penalty for Catiline and his prominent followers. However, a young senator called Gaius Julius Caesar argued against summary execution. In seeking clemency for the conspirators, Caesar came to prominence for the first time.

As the debate went on, Catiline fled to Etruria, only to be killed in battle. Marcus Porcius Cato took the opportunity to turn the senate in Cicero's favor, and the remaining conspirators were executed the same day.

Cicero recognized that Rome desperately needed a period of peace and reconciliation between opposing classes. He contended that the only way to preserve the state was through a *concordia ordinum* (harmony between the classes). More specifically, he sought concord between the two most privileged groups of Roman society—the traditional aristocracy and the business class.

This modern statue depicting the slave rebel Spartacus is located in Sandanski, Bulgaria, which is believed to be the birthplace of Spartacus.

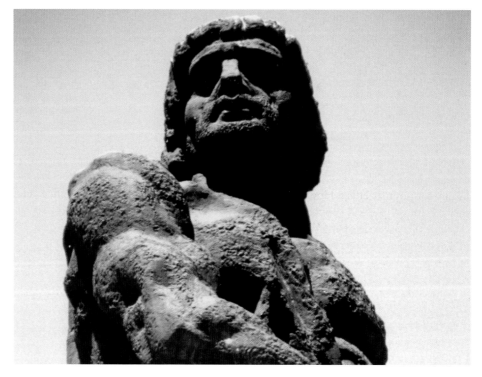

When Pompey returned in triumph from the east in 62 BCE, the senate gave him a great procession. The senate then asked Pompey to disband his army, as the law required of all victorious commanders who might pose a threat to the republic. Much to the senate's relief, he did so. In spite of his compliance, the senate continued to regard Pompey as a serious rival to their own power and failed to ratify the terms he had negotiated in the east or to give land to his troops. Pompey was learning for the second time that his true allies were not the senators, but the plebeians of the people's party. After all he had done for the republic, Pompey was reduced to the role of a defenseless private citizen.

Julius Caesar

Julius Caesar was born into a patrician family and always claimed that he was descended from Aeneas, one of the legendary founders of Rome. After serving in various military campaigns as a young man, Caesar returned to Rome in 63 BCE. He then managed to get himself elected to the position of pontifex maximus—the head of the state religion. This election was a significant political step. Once regarded as the holder of all sacred knowledge, the pontifex maximus had at one time been responsible for the administration of the *jus divinum*—the divine law by which all Rome was governed. By Caesar's time, the position was maintained by a cynical aristocracy primarily for popular effect. However, it still carried great political importance and allowed Caesar to dispense virtually unlimited patronage to ensure his power.

Caesar's rise continued when he was made praetor in 62 BCE. However, debt was a considerable problem; among other people, Caesar owed a large amount of money to Marcus Crassus, who was one of the richest men in Rome. When Caesar was made governor of southern

Spain a year later, his other creditors only let him go after Crassus personally guaranteed the debts. In Spain, however, Caesar did well, amassing riches from the inhabitants in typical Roman fashion. He returned to Rome in 60 BCE more than able to clear all his financial obligations.

Caesar wanted the consulship, but he lacked the power to gain it on his own. His political opponents in the senate were reluctant to grant him a triumphal procession. They did not want him garnering the publicity and popularity that a citywide celebration would bring him. Caesar agreed to forego the triumph, choosing instead to run for office. He was duly elected consul, with the assistance of his old friend Crassus.

The first triumvirate

As consul, Caesar put together an unlikely alliance. Needing the money and influence of Crassus and the soldiers' vote that Pompey could still bring in, Caesar managed to unite Crassus and Pompey in his support. The marriage of

In this 19th-century-CE fresco by Cesare Maccari, Cicero denounces the traitor Catiline in the senate.

The Gallic Wars

Transalpine Gaul, lying between the mountain ranges of the Pyrenees and the Alps, was already a highly Romanized province. However, many tribes in the region were at loggerheads, and they sought Caesar's support in their struggles. He and his legions were only too willing to help, subjugating peoples all the way to the Rhine River.

By the time Caesar had established the Rhine as the northern border of the republic, it had become clear to the squabbling Gauls that they had invited an unwelcome and hungry guest into their midst. However, Caesar only consolidated his victories over the Gauls with considerable difficulty. Rebellions in the province were frequent, and the need to subdue them was almost constant.

Soon, the authorities in Rome began to receive reports, many from Caesar himself, about a war that was winning new territory. Gradually, Pompey and Crassus grew concerned about Caesar's success and his rapidly growing power. The senate shared their concern.

However, Caesar still had an advocate in Rome. The former aristocrat Publius Clodius Pulcher, a fanatical member of the popular party, had assumed the role of a plebeian, replacing his aristocratic name Claudius with the less pretentious Clodius. A fiery public speaker, he used a private army to intimidate those who were not impressed by his words alone. After he was elected tribune in 59 BCE, he set out to settle Caesar's scores with Cicero. The issue raised the following year was an old one—the summary execution of the Catiline conspirators in 63

This Roman coin bears the profile of Julius Caesar. The appearance of Caesar's likeness on coins led to accusations that he wanted to make himself king.

Pompey to Caesar's daughter Julia reinforced the contract. This alliance was a powerful one, especially in view of Caesar's penchant for ignoring any laws he found inconvenient. However, he did ensure that the senate at last ratified Pompey's agreements in the east. Caesar also introduced a bill that would give Pompey's troops grants of land. When this bill was obstructed by both the senate and the popular assembly, Caesar used some of Pompey's veterans to push through the legislation by force of arms. It soon became clear that the triumvirate, not the senate, ruled Rome.

By 58 BCE, Caesar had arranged a special command for himself, the governorship of the provinces of Illyria, Cisalpine Gaul, and Transalpine Gaul. Taking an army with him, Caesar departed for the north.

BCE. Accusing Cicero of acting unconstitutionally, Clodius drove the lawyer into exile.

Clodius's ascendancy did not last. In 57 BCE, he made the mistake of turning on Pompey, subjecting him to virtual house arrest. Pompey retaliated, summoning help from his former troops. Clodius sank swiftly from power, unable to prevent Pompey from arranging for Cicero's return.

The Luca agreement

Relations among the three members of the triumvirate were steadily deteriorating. In 56 BCE, Caesar made a secret trip to Luca, on the Italian Peninsula, where he met his two partners to renegotiate their alliance.

In 55 BCE, while Pompey and Crassus were sharing the consulship, details of the secret agreement came to light. Caesar was to stay in Gaul for another five years, and on his return, he would be guaranteed another consulship and continued army command. Pompey was made commander of Spain but would stay in Rome to carry out his consular duties, delegating his authority in Spain to others. Crassus was made governor of the new province of Syria and equipped with a large army to bring the Parthians there under control. He would continue to be nominal joint consul with Pompey.

The senate was forced to submit to the arrangement. Even the traditionalist Cicero acquiesced, to the point of undertaking to be the spokesman of the alliance. Disillusioned by the failure of the old oligarchy (with its adherence to the rule of law and its system of patrician-dominated government), Cicero took refuge in writing and produced works on philosophy and rhetoric, including *De republica* and *De oratore*. However, he was to remain true to Pompey throughout the forthcoming struggles.

In this 20th-century-CE illustration, the armies of Julius Caesar cross the Rubicon River on their way to Rome.

The collapse of the triumvirate

In 55 BCE, Crassus took his army to Syria, hoping for a military victory that would give him a level of prestige similar to that of Caesar and Pompey. In 53 BCE, Crassus crossed the Euphrates River with 40,000 infantry. However, at the Battle of Carrhae, this force was annihilated by a 10,000-strong Parthian army comprised almost entirely of cavalry. Crassus escaped with a few other survivors and subsequently attempted to negotiate with the Parthians. They agreed to a meeting, but when Crassus arrived at the appointed place, the Parthians murdered him by pouring molten gold down his throat, an ironic reference to his great wealth.

Now, only Caesar and Pompey were left of the original triumvirate, and the ties between them had been weakened when Pompey's wife Julia died in 54 BCE. Caesar's complete conquest of Gaul had given him prestige and wealth almost equal to those of Pompey, and he used them, as Pompey did not, to influence friends and buy support.

Anarchy in Rome

By the end of 53 BCE, chaos reigned in Rome. Gangs, particularly the thugs loyal to Clodius, terrorized the city. The government seemed unable to stop the violence. Only Milo, a supporter of the *optimates* with his own client army, opposed Clodius. Early in 52 BCE, Milo's men killed Clodius in a battle along the Via Appia. Clodius's men then went on a rampage and burned down public buildings in the forum. Because of the rioting, it was impossible to hold elections for the post of praetor. The senate declared a state of emergency and appointed Pompey sole consul, with a special brief to restore order.

Pompey introduced severe laws against civil disorder and used the new laws to convict Milo and other insurgents. Rather than be seen as a would-be dictator, Pompey arranged for Quintus Metellus Scipio, his new father-in-law, to share the consulship with him.

Crossing the Rubicon

Caesar, isolated in Gaul, had two enemies in Rome—Pompey and the senate. Over the course of the next two years, Caesar bargained for his political future and personal safety. During that time, Pompey instigated a number of legal moves that would lessen Caesar's power when he returned to Rome. In 49 BCE, Pompey finally voiced his opposition to Caesar openly, and the senate declared Caesar to be an outlaw.

At that point, Caesar was stationed with his army on the banks of the Rubicon, the river separating Cisalpine Gaul from Italy. Reviewing the situation, Caesar decided to seize the initiative. He crossed the Rubicon and took his army on a fast march to Rome, with the intention of taking power. To this day, the expression "crossing the Rubicon" means taking an irrevocable step.

As city after city fell to Caesar, Pompey fled, first from Rome and then from Italy. He planned to contain Caesar in Italy, but Caesar had other ideas. In another lightning move, Caesar captured Spain and then Massilia from Pompey's generals. On his return to Rome, Caesar was elected consul.

Meanwhile, Pompey had consolidated his forces at Thessalonica in Greece. In 48 BCE, Caesar pursued him there. The two armies met at the Battle of Pharsalus, where Caesar's veteran troops defeated Pompey's larger army. Pompey fled from the field and found refuge, so he thought, in Egypt. However, as soon as he arrived, he met an ignoble death at the hands of an assassin who wanted to ingratiate himself with Caesar. When Caesar followed Pompey to Alexandria, the Egyptians offered him Pompey's head

CLEOPATRA

Cleopatra, the last of the Ptolemaic dynasty in Egypt, was descended from the Macedonian general Ptolemy, who had been appointed governor of Egypt by Alexander the Great. After Alexander's death, Ptolemy took control of the country himself, eventually making himself king of Egypt in 305 BCE. For the 200 years before Cleopatra's birth, Egypt had been allied with Rome. However, as Rome's power increased, the power of the Ptolemies crumbled, until the Egyptians were forced to pay tribute to Rome to preserve their sovereignty.

Cleopatra was born in 69 BCE. She inherited the kingdom on the death of her father, King Ptolemy XII Auletes, in 51 BCE. Cleopatra was 18 years old at the time and ruled jointly with her 12-year-old brother, Ptolemy XIII. She was a charismatic and highly intelligent woman (she could speak nine languages), and she dreamed of making Egypt great again.

Cleopatra's autocratic rule alarmed Ptolemy and his supporters, and by 48 BCE, the two siblings were involved in a struggle for control of the country, Cleopatra fled from Alexandria. Later that year, Ptolemy became involved in the internal politics of Rome when Pompey arrived in Alexandria seeking refuge. Ptolemy had Pompey killed, believing that the gesture would win him favor with Caesar, a belief that proved to be a great mistake.

When Julius Caesar arrived in Egypt a few days later, he was greatly angered by Ptolemy's act.

Meanwhile, Cleopatra had also devised a cunning plan to win over Caesar. Concealed in a rolled-up carpet, she had herself smuggled through enemy lines and delivered to Caesar in the palace. The ruse worked, and the pair soon became lovers.

In the subsequent battle for control of Egypt, Caesar became allied with Cleopatra, and the pair quickly overcame the opposition of Ptolemy, who was killed in 47 BCE. Later that year, Cleopatra gave birth to a son, Caesarion. When Caesar returned to Rome, he took Cleopatra with him. They set up house together, living in great luxury. However, their liaison was cut short when Caesar was assassinated in 44 BCE. Cleopatra, fearing that her life was in danger, hurriedly returned to Egypt.

Cleopatra still hoped to restore Egypt's fortunes, even though the country was on the brink of economic collapse. In 41 BCE, Mark Antony invited her to Tarsus in Anatolia for a political summit. Like Caesar before him, Antony soon began a sexual as well as a political relationship with the Egyptian queen. The pair later married, and Antony moved to Alexandria. After being defeated by the forces of Octavian, the couple committed suicide within a few days of each other in 30 BCE.

This sculpture of Cleopatra dates to the first century BCE, when she ruled Egypt.

This bust depicts the Roman nobleman Marcus Junius Brutus, one of the assassins of Caesar.

Caesar's battles were not yet over. Under the command of Metellus Scipio, troops that were loyal to Pompey held on to the province of Africa. In 46 BCE, Caesar landed eight legions on the African coast and confronted the Pompeian forces at Thapsus. In the ensuing battle, the Pompeian troops were not only defeated but routed, and most of their generals were killed. Marcus Porcius Cato, Caesar's old adversary in the senate, was governor of Utica, just north of Carthage, and rather than fall into Caesar's hands, Cato committed suicide.

Caesar as dictator

In 45 BCE, Caesar returned to Rome as absolute ruler of the republic. A compliant senate appointed him both consul and dictator. This move gave him virtually limitless authority, although his real power depended on his legions. In contrast to Sulla, Caesar carried out almost no reprisals against his defeated enemies. Troops from Pompey's armies were given the option of serving under Caesar, while former political adversaries were given appointments in his administration.

After the years of civil war, preceded by years of incompetent or corrupt administration, Rome was badly in need of a firm, capable hand to restore good governance to the republic. It turned out that Caesar would have less that a year to achieve this. However, he did institute a number of reforms that dramatically changed the way Rome and its provinces were administered.

Rome was a severely overcrowded city, and one of Caesar's first acts was to plan a reconstruction that embraced new public buildings and swept away city slums. Caesar cut back on the handouts of free grain to the poor, on the grounds that the handouts were being misused, and arranged for tens of thousands of poor citizens to be resettled in overseas

on a platter. Caesar was so upset at the sight that he had to avert his eyes.

Caesar in Africa

In Alexandria, the young Ptolemy XIII was in dispute with Cleopatra, his sister, over the succession. Caesar started an affair with Cleopatra, and when he supported her claims against Ptolemy, the king's forces surrounded the palace, imprisoning Caesar. Caesar, narrowly escaping an assassination plot, installed Cleopatra on the throne and defended her position against her younger brother. In the fighting that followed, Ptolemy was killed. Cleopatra, meanwhile, gave birth to a son, named Caesarion.

colonies. Caesar drew up standard regulations for the administration of the municipalities (the self-governed units in Roman territory) and granted Roman citizenship to many previously disenfranchised groups. Above all, he established many new overseas settlements (peopled by his veteran legionnaires) that were all recognized as official Roman colonies. This move changed the nature of the provinces from being merely military conquests to being outposts of the Roman Empire.

Caesar's leniency

At the end of the civil war, people had expected a large-scale cancellation of debts and a redistribution of property. Caesar did confiscate the holdings of some enemies, but he pardoned most enemies and left them in possession of their property. He wanted to be a popular leader, remembered for leniency rather than persecution. Caesar insisted that the statue of Pompey be put back in the senate building after some of his own overzealous followers had pulled it down. He made it clear that he felt Pompey had been a worthy opponent. Caesar also expressed public regret that a man like Cato had taken his own life rather than accept his pardon.

In 45 BCE, Caesar was forced to take his legions abroad once more, this time to Spain to quell a rebellion organized by Pompey's sons, Gnaeus and Sextus Pompeius. The forces met at the Battle of Munda. The battle was hard fought, but Caesar was ultimately victorious. The Pompeians were slaughtered. Gnaeus was killed in the fighting, while Sextus was forced to flee.

Cleopatra and Octavian by the 17th-century-CE Italian painter Il Guercino depicts the Egyptian queen kneeling before the Roman general.

This second-century-CE mosaic depicts two gladiators fighting. Gladiatorial contests were a popular form of entertainment in the first century BCE.

In Rome, the senate heaped honors upon Caesar. His portrait was put on coins, and many statues of him were erected throughout the city. The increasingly autocratic nature of Caesar's rule made his political opponents uneasy. Many feared that he aimed to make himself king—an idea detested in the republic. At the Lupercalia festival in February of 44 BCE, Caesar's lieutenant Mark Antony offered him a golden coronet, the ancient symbol of a king's power. It was obvious from the audience's reaction that this was a very unpopular move. Caesar refused to accept the crown, leading to speculation about whether the whole scene had been staged to make his rejection of kingship clear or whether he

would have accepted the coronet if he had been acclaimed by the public.

The ides of March

In March, May, July, and December, under Caesar's new calendar (see box, page 70), the 15th day was called the ides. The ides of March of 44 BCE proved to be a turning point in history. Opposition to Caesar's power had solidified into a conspiracy of some 60 men, led by Brutus and Cassius, both of whom had fought on Pompey's side and been pardoned by Caesar. In spite of warnings from a soothsayer to "beware the ides of March," Caesar, unprotected by any bodyguard, attended the senate house on the 15th and was stabbed to death. As the body of Caesar lay at the foot of Pompey's statue, the senate panicked. The plotters themselves fled in disorder, wandering around the city with bloodstained clothes and daggers.

Caesar had named Mark Antony as his executor, and Antony used the position to gain popular support. At the funeral, Antony read out Caesar's will before an immense crowd assembled in front of the senate. The dictator had left his gardens to the state and a moderate amount of money (300 sesterces) to every citizen. When they heard this, the crowd went wild. Antony also publicly named those responsible for the murder and brandished Caesar's bloodstained toga to whip up the crowd still further. The result of Antony's speech was that popular sentiment swung fiercely against the conspirators, who found themselves in mortal danger.

Octavian

Caesar's sudden death created a power vacuum in Rome. However, the person who took greatest advantage of this situation was not Mark Antony, but Octavian, Caesar's great-nephew and adopted son and heir. Not yet 20, Octavian proved a formidable political operator. He commanded loyalty from Caesar's old party, some members of which defected from Antony to him. Octavian also found support in the senate, in particular from Cicero, who delivered a series of orations against Antony, representing him as an enemy of ancient Roman freedoms.

In a compromise agreement, the conspirators Cassius and Brutus were pardoned by the senate. However, they were not safe in Rome, and by 43 BCE, they had fled to the eastern provinces, where they set about raising armies. Back in

The suicide of the Egyptian queen Cleopatra has been a popular subject for artists. This 17th-century-CE painting is by Guido Cagnacci.

ANCIENT ROME

THE JULIAN CALENDAR

One of Julius Caesar's most enduring legacies was the calendar revision made during his term of office as pontifex maximus. In the original Roman calendar, a year consisted of 355 days, with an extra month added every other year. Caesar was advised by the Alexandrian scholar Sosigenes that the length of the year should theoretically be 365.25 days. Caesar then introduced a new calendar where years consisted of 365 days, with an extra day (the 29th of February) added every four years to make up the difference. The end of February was chosen for the extra day because the Romans originally celebrated the new year on the first day of March.

This Julian calendar survived intact until the 16th century CE, when it was replaced by the Gregorian calendar. The reason for the change was that Sosigenes had slightly miscalculated the length of the year; he was off by 11 minutes and 14 seconds. This error caused the dates of the seasons to change. The problem was rectified by declaring that no century year should be a leap year unless it is divisible by 400.

Rome, the senate turned against Antony, who was now at the head of an army in Cisalpine Gaul. The senate declared Antony's occupation of the area to be illegal and dispatched Octavian, together with the consuls Aulus Hirtius and Vibius Pansa, to Mutina, where Antony was defeated. Antony then withdrew his forces to Transalpine Gaul, where he succeeded in attracting the provincial governors to his cause.

The two elderly consuls both died at the Battle of Mutina, leaving Octavian in sole command of the army. Increasingly out of favor with the senate, Octavian marched on Rome to demand the consulship by force. Once he had been appointed consul, Octavian annulled the pardons that had given to the conspirators. Because Brutus and Cassius were in command of large armies, this daring move was tantamount to a declaration of war.

To strengthen his own hand, Octavian made overtures to Antony and met him and Lepidus (a commander of seven legions that had served under Caesar) for a peace conference at Bononia. The three agreed to form the second triumvirate—the *triumviri rei publicae constituendae* (the board of three to settle the constitution). In effect, this was a military dictatorship.

The second triumvirate

Antony sealed the compact by marrying Octavian's sister, Octavia. The new triumvirate then set about issuing banishment lists, as Sulla had done. This move allowed them to seize a victim's property and put him to death. Hundreds of senators and thousands of *equites* were massacred. One of the early victims was Cicero, now an old man of 63, who was denounced by Antony.

In 42 BCE, the armies of Antony and Octavian met those of Brutus and Cassius at the Battle of Philippi and defeated them. Both Cassius and Brutus committed suicide rather than fall into their enemies' hands. The Roman world was then divided among the members of the triumvirate. Octavian received the west, Antony received the east, and Lepidus received Africa. Their only remaining adversary was Pompey's son Sextus. He was now based in Sicily and had command of a powerful fleet, which he used to blockade supplies of goods

70

destined for Rome, reducing the city to a state of near starvation.

In 36 BCE, Octavian defeated Sextus in a sea battle off Sicily. Lepidus made an abortive attempt to claim Sicily for himself, but when his troops deserted him, he was left powerless. Octavian stripped Lepidus of his membership in the triumvirate and his rule of Africa and banished him to a town on the Italian Peninsula. Only two members of the triumvirate remained—Octavian and Antony.

Antony and Cleopatra

After a campaign in Parthia, Antony returned to Alexandria and resumed his relationship with Cleopatra, which had started in 41 BCE. Cleopatra was ambitious and hoped that her son by Julius Caesar would one day rule Rome. She persuaded Antony to marry her (even though he was still married to Octavia), and he set up his base of operations in the Egyptian port of Alexandria.

In Rome, Octavian used Antony's actions as the basis for a propaganda campaign against him. Although Antony made counterclaims against Octavian, public opinion, especially among the Roman upper class, was on Octavian's side. In 33 BCE, the triumvirate was officially terminated. The following year, rumors that Antony planned to make Cleopatra the queen of Rome further hardened opinion against him. Octavian was made consul, and the senate declared war on Egypt.

As both sides prepared for conflict, Antony and Cleopatra equipped a fleet of more than 500 ships, which they sailed across the Mediterranean and into the Adriatic Sea. In 31 BCE, they were engaged in battle by the Roman fleet, commanded by Agrippa, at Actium on the west coast of Greece. The encounter was a total humiliation for Antony. Shortly after the start of the battle, Cleopatra left the rest of the fleet in her flagship and was followed by Antony. Believing that Antony had simply run away, the rest of the fleet—and his land army—capitulated without a fight.

Octavian's pursuit was interrupted by a mutiny that necessitated a return to Italy, but he did finally reach Alexandria in 30 BCE. With no army left to defend him, Antony took his own life. Cleopatra followed suit a few days later. To put an end to any further claims from the Ptolemaic dynasty, Octavian killed Caesarion and the eldest of Antony's sons by Cleopatra. Octavian then made Egypt a Roman province. Having vanquished all opposition, Octavian returned to Rome in triumph.

See also:

The Age of Augustus (page 72) • Revolution and Reform (page 44)

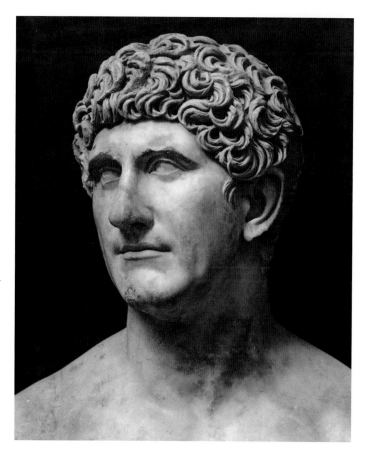

This bust depicts the Roman general Mark Antony, a member of the second triumvirate.

71

THE AGE OF AUGUSTUS

After the civil wars that had ravaged the republic in the mid-first century BCE, Rome enjoyed a prolonged period of relative peace. The man responsible for overseeing this era was Caesar Augustus, the first Roman emperor.

After the deaths of Antony and Cleopatra in 30 BCE, Octavian (63 BCE–14 CE) was left as the most powerful man in the Roman world. He remained so for the next 44 years. The form of government he established in the new Roman Empire was called the principate, and it remained essentially unchanged for 200 years. During the period of his rule, Octavian became known as Augustus Caesar, a title bestowed upon him by the senate (see box, page 74).

Even though Augustus effectively controlled Rome, he was careful to keep in place old Roman institutions such as the senate and the consulship. This move was partially a pragmatic one; if he had dismantled these political bodies and positions, he would have opened himself to accusations that he was seeking kingship. However, there is also evidence that Augustus genuinely believed in many of the principles upon which the Roman republic was founded. Nevertheless, he knew that fundamental changes were needed if the Roman Empire was to function smoothly.

During his rule, Augustus brought peace to the lands conquered by his predecessors. He embarked on an ambitious building program in Rome, and under his rule, literature and the arts flourished. Roman political and administrative systems spread throughout the empire, thereby consolidating Rome's central authority. Meanwhile, the Roman Empire continued to expand through military means as the subjugation of Spain was completed and new regions were brought under Roman control in Germany and the Balkans.

A new Rome

The Rome that Augustus returned to in 29 BCE badly needed the restoration of law and order, as well as a stable government that would override the turmoil caused by aristocratic intrigue and personal ambition. Augustus had more than enough military power to enforce order, but he preferred to legitimize his power by using the traditional forms of government. One way in which he did so was by holding the consulship. Augustus was reelected consul on his return from the east and was reelected year after year until 23 BCE, when he declined to run for the office.

Augustus was also awarded various special powers during the course of his rule. In 27 BCE, Augustus voluntarily relinquished the extraordinary powers he had assumed during the civil war against Antony and returned them to the senate and the people. However, in return, he was awarded various special titles. Most importantly, Augustus was given a 10-year tenure of the provinces of Gaul,

This bronze head, depicting the emperor Augustus, dates to around 25 BCE and was found in Sudan. Archaeologists believe the figure was stolen during a raid on Roman Egypt.

OCTAVIAN'S TITLES

In 27 BCE, Octavian was awarded two new titles by the senate. The first, Augustus, was the name by which he became universally known. The word is difficult to translate, but it is derived from the Latin word *augere*, meaning "to increase." The title indicated Augustus's authority over the rest of the Roman population.

Augustus's full title was Augustus Caesar. Augustus and his successors put great emphasis on their descent from Julius Caesar, and the name lived on in medieval Europe and into the 20th century. The German title Kaiser and the Russian Czar both derive from the Roman name.

The second title bestowed upon Augustus by the senate in 27 BCE was *princeps*, meaning "first citizen." Augustus preferred this title because it offered a connotation of legitimacy. Under this title, Augustus presented himself as the first servant of the empire, in keeping with the long-standing Roman tradition of public service. Augustus was not the first prominent political figure to have been awarded this title—Caesar's old enemy Pompey had also been *princeps*.

Augustus liked the trappings of civilian authority. During his time as *princeps*, he held a number of traditional civilian offices. However, in contrast to previous holders, Augustus often held several offices simultaneously and without the traditional time limits.

Spain, and Syria. It was in these three regions that Augustus's troops were based, so this move legitimized his military power. Later, Augustus was also given tribunal power for life. This honor allowed him to convene the senate, propose motions before it, and veto decisions made by either the senate or the popular assembly. Augustus was also given a number of powers traditionally associated with the position of censor; those powers included the rights to conduct a census and to control the composition of the senate. No senator served without Augustus's approval.

The senate

Despite the restrictions on its power, Augustus was anxious to maintain the senate because he saw it as the embodiment of Roman tradition. He worked hard to maintain cordial relations with the body and to preserve the illusion of consultation with it. In an effort to rid the senate of those he considered

This coin bearing the profile of Augustus was found in Germany at the site of the Battle of Teutoburg Forest.

unworthy, Augustus cut its numbers from around 1,000 to around 600. To bring the senate numbers back up to strength, he promoted a number of members of the equestrian class, who had previously been barred from holding senatorial office. Augustus also established a minimum annual income requirement (one million sesterces) for becoming a senator, reasoning that if the senate's new members were no longer required to be of adequate rank at birth, at least they would be of adequate means.

The senate was given new tasks. It was charged with the day-to-day running of both Rome and the rest of the Italian Peninsula, as well as several provinces of limited strategic impor-

tance. The latter were generally referred to as the public provinces. The governors of these provinces were selected by lot from among the senators, who were required to serve a one-year term without any military backup.

The imperial provinces

Augustus retained personal control of all non-public provinces, which were called the imperial provinces. He alone appointed their governors, who served as long as he pleased rather than for a set time period. These provinces might have a garrison. Sometimes, *equites* who were not members of the senate were appointed to the governorship of imperial provinces. For example, the equestrian Pontius Pilate

Alexandria, the ruins of which are shown here, was the main port of the Roman province of Egypt. Egypt was annexed during the reign of Augustus.

This marble statue of Augustus dates to the first century CE. It is a copy of an earlier statue that was made during his lifetime.

was the governor of the province of Judaea at the time of the crucifixion of Jesus Christ.

The most important imperial province commanded by an equestrian governor was Egypt, with its vast Ptolemaic treasure and its grain supply. So valuable was Egypt that troops were stationed there when no other equestrian governor was allowed to have legions.

Following the example of Julius Caesar, Augustus established many colonies throughout his empire. These colonies were populated by veteran soldiers. In these settlements, every citizen was a Roman citizen, and the forms of civil government were modeled on those of Rome. This vast network of more than 100 colonies helped to spread Roman culture to the farthest reaches of the empire.

Another type of provincial settlement was the *civitas*. *Civitates* were self-governing, autonomous communities consisting entirely of non-Roman citizens. They existed under the protection of the provincial governor, and paid taxes to Rome. As they became increasingly Latinized, their status might be changed to that of *municipia* (municipal town). In the *municipia*, townspeople who assumed public office might be accorded Roman citizenship. All the provinces paid tribute to Rome. This

money was spent on military protection, the expanding civil service, and the extensive public works that were increasingly being initiated by Augustus.

The new Rome

Despite its great number of inhabitants, Rome still had the look of an old walled *oppidum* (fortified town) grown beyond its boundaries. The city was crowded and dirty, and many of its public buildings were in a state of disrepair. The forum, the center of Roman public life, was much too small. Augustus set about giving Rome the outward splendor he felt it deserved. "I found a city of stone, and I will leave behind a city of marble," he boasted. He proved good to his word.

Augustus ordered marble temples to be built in the center of the city, and he replaced the old forum with a new one nearby. Augustus also built improved access roads to the city and had the Tiber River dredged in an attempt to stop its annual flooding.

Augustus made moves to protect the people of Rome against famine. In the past, a foreign enemy needed only to control the sea to be able to starve Rome. As a preventive measure, Augustus established an administration to control the grain supply and organized annual imports from Egypt. He also made distributions of grain to the masses, a move that increased his personal popularity.

76

Urban safety in Rome

In the slums of Rome, the inhabitants frequently fell victim to marauding gangs, who found plenty of places to hide in the noisome alleyways. The final days of the republic had also seen serious rioting. Augustus attempted to address some of these problems by forming a police force, which consisted of four cohorts of special troops under a leader called the *praefectus urbi* (prefect of the city), who became one of the most powerful men in Rome. This force of trained riot police appears to have been relatively effective.

In addition to the police force, Augustus appointed 7,000 night watchmen, whose job was to look out for fires or any cases of crime after dark. The night watchmen were led by a *praefectus vigilum* (prefect of the watchers). While neither of these initiatives made the streets of Rome completely free of danger, there was a distinct improvement in urban safety.

Traditional family values

Augustus also set about restoring traditional family values. To counteract what he saw as the lax morality of the citizen-

This fresco decorates the wall of a villa that once belonged to Augustus's wife Livia.

This bust depicts Julia, the daughter of Augustus. Julia scandalized Rome with her promiscuous behavior.

and divorce, was married three times. His first wife was Clodia Pulchra, the stepdaughter of Mark Antony. Augustus married Clodia in order to cement his original political alliance with Antony but divorced her in 40 BCE. Augustus then married Scribonia, a woman who was older than himself. She had previously been the wife of two consuls and had a child by each of them. In 38 BCE, Augustus divorced Scribonia for Livia, the wife of the elderly Tiberius Claudius Nero, who was persuaded to agree to a divorce.

Augustus brought up his daughter Julia (by Scribonia) and his granddaughter of the same name very strictly, requiring daily reports on their progress and behavior. However, once they had grown up and were beyond his control, their promiscuous escapades scandalized Rome. Augustus eventually banished them from the city.

Literature

In this new era of peace and prosperity, Roman literature blossomed as never before. It became the fashion for writers to give public readings from their works in progress, a practice that greatly increased their potential reading public. Under the patronage of both Augustus and his friend Maecenas, several Roman writers came to the fore. These men, who were to claim lasting places in world literature, included the heroic poet Virgil (see box, page 80), the witty cultural pundit Horace, and the historian Livy.

One writer who fell out of favor with Augustus was the poet Ovid. He specialized in lighthearted verses, some of which made comments on contemporary society. He also recounted many of the Greek myths in verse form. However, Ovid offended Augustus by publishing erotic poetry and by becoming involved in a

ry, he introduced chastity laws. Illicit lovers faced banishment, property confiscation, and a ban on any future marriage. Because he considered the ideal family to consist of a father, mother, and as many children as possible, Augustus established a law called the *lex iulia*. This law conferred privileges on married couples with children and imposed civil restrictions on single people and the childless. Other laws made marriage easier (even if the parents of the bride and bridegroom objected) and divorce harder. These measures were intended to provide Rome with a population of moral, responsible citizens. However, the laws had limited effect.

Augustus, who did not consider himself subject to his own laws on marriage scandal with Julia, the emperor's daughter. Augustus banished Ovid to Tomi on the Black Sea, where Ovid's poetic imagination continued to flourish in exile. He wrote flattering verses to Augustus in the hope of being recalled to his beloved Rome. However, these efforts were to no avail; Ovid died in Tomi in 17 CE.

Religion

During the years of civil war, the Romans' interest in the state religion had waned. Augustus now sought to revive it. He replaced the crumbling temples that had fallen into disuse and erected the great rectangular Pantheon as a temple to all the gods. He met personally with the priests of all the Roman colleges to encourage them to restore the religious rituals. In 17 BCE, Augustus revived the festival of the *ludi saeculares* (secular games), turning it into an occasion to give thanks for deliverance from a dangerous past and to welcome a new era of peace. For three days, sporting events by day alternated with feasts and torchlit processions by night, all intended to signal the restoration of Rome's greatness. The poet Horace composed a celebratory hymn that was sung before a new shrine to Apollo on the Palatine Hill, and then Augustus made a sacrifice to the gods.

Augustus himself later began to be worshipped as a god. In the eastern cities, it was not uncommon to deify rulers, so it was no surprise that cults arose to worship Augustus. He did nothing to stop the practice, because it only served to reinforce his authority. Soon, he was being worshipped in many towns on the Italian Peninsula. Special colleges were set up for this purpose. Their priests were generally freed slaves who made a career of this worshipping. While the custom was not formally introduced in Rome, Augustus did build a shrine to his guardian spirit in every neighborhood. However, he was not formally deified until after his death.

The pax Augusta

The personal loyalty of the army was vital to Augustus. Each year, on the first day of January, every soldier swore an oath of allegiance to him. Because Augustus bore the name of the deified Julius Caesar, the support pledged to him carried the weight of a religious vow.

The Roman poet Horace, depicted here in a 16th-century-CE fresco, was just one of a number of writers to flourish under Augustus.

VIRGIL

Like many of his contemporaries, the poet Virgil (70–19 BCE) modeled his first literary works on those of earlier Greek writers. One early collection of pastoral poems, the *Eclogues*, were influenced by Theocritus. Virgil's *Georgics*, which purported to be a practical guide to farming and husbandry, was actually a song of praise to nature and the charms of rural life.

Virgil's greatest work, however, was the epic poem the *Aeneid*, which made him famous both in his own time and throughout posterity.

Emulating Homer's epic tales, the *Iliad* and the *Odyssey*, the *Aeneid* tells the story of Aeneas, a survivor from the Trojan War, who makes his way to Italy and eventually founds Rome. The *Aeneid* glorified the history of Rome, and the feelings of civic pride that it inspired meant that it encapsulated the optimistic spirit of the Augustan age.

The poem was unfinished on Virgil's death, and the poet's dying wish was for it to be burned. However, Augustus himself intervened and ordered the poem to be saved.

This statue depicts Ovid, one of the greatest of all Roman poets. He fell out of favor with Augustus and was banished from Rome.

To allay fears of a military dictatorship, Augustus had partially demobilized his army after the Battle of Actium in 30 BCE, reducing the number of legions from 60 to 28. It now constituted a permanent standing army of around 300,000 men. Augustus also maintained a marine corps on the imperial fleet and had his own personal bodyguard, called the praetorian cohorts.

Within each legion, the officers were all Roman citizens. The top ranks (the legates and tribunes) were either senators or *equites*. Below them were the centurions, who were typically Roman citizens from municipal towns.

The army played an important part in the consolidation of the empire, quite apart from any military conquests. Many Roman encampments were created to maintain a military presence in an area. These settlements replicated the Roman lifestyle, and they frequently developed into permanent societies of their own. Over the centuries, some of them grew into major European cities.

Although it was illegal for a soldier to marry, many of them fathered children who were subsequently granted Roman citizenship. Retiring soldiers often settled in the region where they had been assigned. Augustus encouraged this trend, granting the retired soldiers free land to form new colonies.

New territory

Under Augustus, the Roman Empire acquired new territory very slowly. In Spain, it took years of fighting to subdue the last recalcitrant tribes. When victory was finally achieved, several new colonies were established. The present-day city of Saragossa (originally called Caesar Augusta) emerged from one of them.

In the east, meanwhile, Augustus's generals ensured the security of Roman possessions in Syria and Anatolia. However, civil war in Armenia threatened the stability of the region. Both the Romans and the Parthians fanned the flames of this war by supporting different pretenders to the throne. The situation dragged on for years; at one time, a Roman candidate secured the throne, and at another time, a Parthian candidate did. Augustus made the pragmatic decision not to engage in a potentially costly military confrontation. In 20 BCE, Augustus's stepson and future successor, Tiberius, negotiated a peace treaty with the Parthians.

In the Balkans, Roman power spread as far as the Danube River. Roman military successes in this region eventually yielded three new provinces, Moesia, Pannonia and Dalmatia.

In this 16th-century-CE painting by Federico Barocci, Aeneas carries his father Anchises from the burning city of Troy. The poet Virgil's account of the story of Aeneas was written during the reign of Augustus.

*The **Ara Pacis Augustae** was created in 13 BCE to celebrate the return of Augustus to Rome after campaigns in Gaul and Spain.*

At the same time that new provinces were being acquired in the Balkans, Roman influence was being extended in present-day Germany. In 11 BCE, the general Nero Claudius Drusus confronted German tribes who had been conducting raids into northern Gaul and defeated them at the Battle of the Lupia River. Over the course of the next two years, he managed to extend Roman control as far east as the Elbe River. However, Roman dominance of the German peoples who lived between the Rhine and the Elbe was superficial and did not last.

Toward the end of his reign, Augustus appointed a new provincial governor, Varus, to the Rhine region. The harshness of Varus's rule prompted a revolt. The German tribes united under a young chieftain named Arminius, who had been a soldier in the Roman army.

In 9 CE, Arminius lured Varus and his three legions into an area of forests and marshes, where traditional Roman military tactics would not work. The German chieftain was then able to overcome the Roman armies and almost completely annihilate them.

The Battle of Teutoburg Forest was one of the biggest disasters in Roman military history. When the news reached Rome, Augustus is reputed to have cried: "Varus, Varus, give me back my legions!" Later attempts to reestablish Roman control east of the Rhine proved unsuccessful, and the river became the northern boundary of the Roman Empire in mainland Europe.

The succession

Augustus ruled Rome for more than 40 years, and during that time, the empire enjoyed an unparalleled period of prosperity and relative peace. However, in one vital area, Augustus had not been successful. In spite of three marriages, he failed to produce a son. As his health deteriorated, it became imperative that he should nominate his successor. Augustus's first choice, in 13 BCE, was Agrippa, his son-in-law and former classmate. However, within a year of his appointment, Agrippa died.

Augustus's next choice was his stepson Tiberius, who had been one of Augustus's most talented and successful generals. In 12 BCE, Augustus forced Tiberius to divorce his beloved wife, Vipsania, and marry Agrippa's widow, Julia. Resentful at this interference in his personal life, Tiberius retreated to the island of Rhodes, where he lived for the next seven years in isolated retirement. This experience seems to have nurtured feelings of mistrust and pessimism that would return in later life.

Augustus then favored Agrippa's two eldest sons, Gaius and Lucius Caesar, for the succession, but by 4 BCE, both were dead. Augustus had no choice but to turn back to Tiberius. Later that year, Tiberius was recalled from Rhodes to be officially adopted by Augustus.

In the following years, Tiberius was appointed to various political positions, and in 13 CE, he was given powers equal to Augustus. Later that year, Augustus left his will at the House of the Vestals in Rome, together with an account of his life's work called *Res Gestae Divi Augusti* (The Achievements of the Divine Augustus). When Augustus died in August of 14 CE, Tiberius became emperor without any opposition.

See also:

The End of the Republic (page 56) • The Julio-Claudian Emperors (page 84)

*This relief from the **Ara Pacis Augustae** depicts a procession of senators.*

THE JULIO-CLAUDIAN EMPERORS

Augustus's successors enlarged the empire to its greatest extent and secured its borders. They centralized the collection of taxes and all other administration in the hands of the imperial authority located in the city of Rome.

After Augustus died in 14 CE, the senate declared him a god, a traditional Roman way of honoring dead leaders. In his place, Augustus had nominated his adopted son Tiberius, who had originally been his stepson.

The Roman constitution did not include a right of succession to the throne, but Augustus's personal prestige ensured that Tiberius would receive the support of the senate. For some years, Tiberius had been the emperor's co-ruler, gaining experience of imperial leadership to make his succession more secure.

The concept of succession became a tradition, but the throne was not simply passed from father to son—as became common in later monarchies. During his lifetime, each emperor sought a suitable candidate—usually a member of the imperial family—whom he then adopted as his son. Tiberius adopted a great-grandson of Augustus, Gaius (called Caligula), but Caligula nominated his uncle, Claudius I. Claudius was succeeded by his stepson Nero, who was also a descendant of Augustus by marriage. These four related successors, together with Augustus, comprise what is called the Julio-Claudian dynasty.

The absence of a law that established which of an emperor's relatives had the right to succession could be disastrous. Any ambitious person with enough influence could aspire to be emperor, with or without the support of the public. As a result, few members of the imperial family died a natural death. Every emperor lived in constant fear of conspiracies hatched among the counselors, favorites, and administrators who surrounded him. The atmosphere at court was full of suspicion and intrigue. While a career as a public servant offered unprecedented opportunity, it also presented unprecedented danger.

Tiberius

Tiberius came to power in 14 CE at age 56, having lived most of his life in the shadow of Augustus. His personal life was unrewarding, and he could be moody and difficult. However, he proved to be a meticulous administrator of the imperial treasury. He cut back on public expenses to such an extent that he lost much support among Rome's citizens, who had expected spectacular celebrations and generous grain handouts from their new emperor.

Tiberius also had a poor reputation among contemporary historians such as Tacitus, who described Tiberius as an unapproachable ruler who despised his subjects. Modern historians tend to be more positive, pointing out that the bureaucracy of the empire ran smoothly under Tiberius. Like Augustus, Tiberius

This contemporary, life-size marble bust is a portrait of Nero, probably the most notorious emperor of the Julio-Claudian dynasty.

the ability to administer the empire alone. Worse, his great power and his intolerance meant that few people were brave enough to give him advice or offer an honest opinion about his actions. According to one story, when Tiberius made his first appearance in the senate as *princeps*, a fool-hardy senator asked him, "Caesar, which portion of power do you want to reserve for yourself?" When Tiberius was clearly irritated, the alarmed senator hurriedly added: "I say this because we cannot go on without the unity of leadership and power in your hands."

A trusted ally

Tiberius was said to trust only one man in the empire: Sejanus, the leader of the Praetorian Guard. This body of elite soldiers served as the imperial bodyguard. Its men were stationed around the palace in Rome and at other strategic locations throughout the Italian Peninsula. Only a trusted confidant of the emperor was appointed to be commander of the guard.

It soon became obvious to everyone except the emperor that Sejanus wanted to exploit the emperor's trust to have himself designated as the imperial successor. He acquired influence over Tiberius and implicated the emperor's relatives in plots so that, one by one, Tiberius eliminated his relatives on charges of treason. Sejanus's influence continued to grow, and in 26 CE, the aging Tiberius retreated to the island of Capri, leaving imperial control in the hands of the prefect of Rome.

Sejanus remained near Rome with most of the guard. He functioned as a caretaker and protector for Tiberius, censoring the news received by the

did not strain the imperial resources trying to extend the empire. Therefore, only those in his immediate vicinity had to fear the emperor's paranoia.

The dangers of power

It was under Tiberius that the dangers of placing absolute power in the hands of one man became increasingly clear. The emperor did not delegate responsibility to his advisers, but neither did he have emperor. The senate could only watch as Sejanus misused the power that Tiberius increasingly delegated to him. Eventually, a number of senators protested to Tiberius, letting it be known that they would oppose him if Sejanus was not removed. The commander panicked and made hasty plans for a coup, which was perhaps what his opponents had wanted. When Tiberius heard of the plot, he acted promptly, sending word to the senate demanding Sejanus's execution. The soldier and his supporters were put to death for treason in 31 CE.

A paranoid emperor

Senators who hoped the elimination of Sejanus would improve matters were disappointed. Betrayal by his closest confidant only intensified Tiberius's paranoia. Suspicious of everyone, he began to show signs of mental illness. He remained on Capri, conducting imperial business by letter. Meanwhile, rumors circulated in Rome that the emperor was spending his time in orgies or enjoying cruel entertainments.

Other rumors said that Tiberius had arranged for the murder of his nephew and heir apparent, Germanicus. The son of Tiberius's brother Drusus, who had died on campaign in Germany, Germanicus was a man of great personal charm who had led several successful military campaigns. However, Tiberius hated and mistrusted him. When Germanicus died in the east after a short illness, it was generally suspected that Piso, the governor of Syria, had poisoned him at Tiberius's instigation.

Tiberius's continued self-imposed exile on Capri was a source of much uncertainty and suspicion in Rome. Senators who had been discredited by Sejanus found that the emperor's trust in them was not restored. New plots and conspiracies abounded, and Tiberius received plenty of information about

This marble portrait of Tiberius was carved in 4 CE to celebrate the future emperor's adoption by Augustus.

them from *delatores* (informers). In a judicial system without public prosecutors, it was left to private citizens to make accusations in court. If someone were convicted of treason, his estate was confiscated and one quarter of its value was awarded to the man who had denounced him. Consequently, an entire profession of *delatores* arose in Rome. Once an informer had accused someone, that individual had little chance of clearing

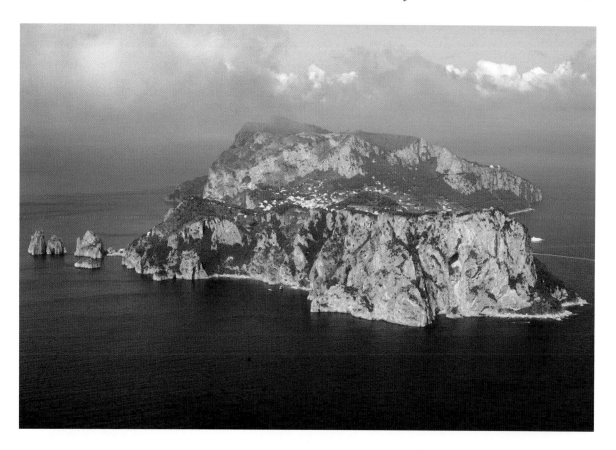

his name. His friends would not dare to help him, and indeed, they often endorsed the condemnation to save their own lives. The last few years of Tiberius's life were a reign of terror, and it was with a feeling of relief that Rome learned of his death in 37 CE at the age of 77. He was not deified as Caesar and Augustus had been before him.

"Little Boots"

At his death, Tiberius left two adult heirs: his grandson Tiberius Gemellus and his great-nephew Gaius, whom he had adopted as a son. The senate immediately recognized the latter as the successor, although little was known about him. As the son of the popular Germanicus, however, it was reported that the soldiers adored him. As a child, Gaius had accompanied his father on campaign and had worn miniature uniforms. This act had

given rise to his nickname, Caligula, meaning "Little Boots."

Caligula was only 25 when he became emperor in 37 CE, and the first few months of his reign came as a breath of fresh air to the hard-pressed Roman citizenry. The *delatores* were persecuted, political prisoners were given an amnesty, and the new *princeps* distinguished himself by his great generosity in laying on spectacular entertainments to amuse the populace. However, seven months into his reign Caligula became ill, and when he recovered, he seemed to have undergone a change of personality. His behavior became capricious and cruel; it was rumored that he had gone mad.

The treason trials resumed, and in 38 CE, Caligula arranged for the executions of his cousin Tiberius Gemellus and Macro, the prefect of the Praetorian Guard who had virtually put Caligula on

Tiberius spent the last decade of his life in exile on the island of Capri, which is located in the Bay of Naples. During that time, he built a succession of luxurious villas on the island to support his self-indulgent lifestyle.

the throne. Caligula squandered the resources that Tiberius had so carefully hoarded. To replace them, Caligula confiscated the estates of wealthy Roman citizens. He humiliated members of the senate and was even said to have made his horse a consul, although modern historians tend to discount the story.

Caligula had himself deified while he was still alive and had altars to himself put up all over the empire. He built a link from his palace on the Palatine Hill in Rome to the temples on the Capitoline, so that, he said, he could communicate more easily with the god Jupiter.

An unpredictable emperor

This divine mania threatened a serious conflict with the Jews in Judaea. Major rebellion was only averted by the local governor's decision to keep ignoring the emperor's order that Caligula be worshipped in the temple in Jerusalem.

The ordinary people of Rome, too, suffered under Caligula. On one occasion, when he was displeased with the crowd watching games in the stadium, the emperor had the games stopped, the sunshades removed, and the exits sealed off by soldiers. For the whole day, he left thousands of spectators sitting in the burning sun without food or drink. Even life could depend on the emperor's whim. He is reported to have said to one of his courtesans, "What a lovely neck! One word from me and it will fly off."

Caligula's unpredictable behavior extended to his treatment of the army. In 40 CE, he marched into Gaul, plundering the countryside. He then gathered his troops in battle array on the beaches of Normandy, as if they were about to be sent to invade Britain. However, when

This statue of Caligula was carved in the first century CE. Excavations at Caligula's palace in Rome have confirmed ancient reports that the building was linked to a temple.

Caligula issued his order, it was to gather seashells! Afterward, Caligula boasted that he had conquered the ocean.

After four years of such imperial behavior, even the Praetorian Guard had had enough. In January of 41 CE, the tribune of the Praetorian Guard, with several others, stabbed Caligula to death in the palace grounds. The conspirators hoped to restore the republic, but other Praetorians intervened.

An unusual succession

While soldiers were looting the palace, they saw a pair of feet behind a curtain. They pulled the cloth away and found Claudius, the terrified uncle of the murdered emperor. Claudius feared that he was going to die too, but the soldiers recognized him as the brother of their former general, Germanicus.

Believing that their own futures depended on who held the principate,

they carried Claudius away to an inner courtyard, where they received him officially as the new emperor. Relieved to have his life spared, Claudius promised them all a generous bounty for their personal allegiance.

Claudius I

Claudius, the grandson of Livia (third wife of Augustus) and a nephew of Tiberius, was born in 10 BCE. He had physical infirmities and a stammer. These disabilities led him to avoid public notice and devote himself to scholarship (see box, page 92). Despite these drawbacks and his age (he was older than 50 at the time of his accession), Claudius proved to be an effective, but controversial, emperor.

The new emperor reorganized the administration of the government, particularly in regard to financial affairs. As had been the custom since the time of Augustus, Claudius managed the empire

Caligula is assassinated by the Praetorian Guard in this illustration from an 18th-century-CE edition of **The History of the Jewish People**, *written by Josephus Flavius around 30 years after the killing.*

Claudius was a scholarly and effective emperor who was nevertheless highly unpopular with his subjects.

as had been outlined for it by Augustus. A strong advocate of the liberal granting of Roman citizenship to imperial subjects in conquered territories, Claudius also appointed people from the provinces to the senate. He gave them whatever rank he chose, instead of having them ascend through the ranks. To avoid offense, Claudius raised many existing senators to patrician status. However, the senate was not happy when in 47 CE he appointed himself to the hitherto defunct office of censor. The position gave him the power to add senators at whim—and to execute them at whim, on trumped up charges of conspiracy or violating state security.

In the provinces, Claudius followed a policy of Romanization, or assimilating other peoples into the empire. This act tended to reduce the importance of the Italian Peninsula in the senate, a fact that did not add to his popularity there. On the peninsula itself, however, Claudius improved government administration within the municipal towns, drained marshes, and built numerous roads and ports. He was responsible for the great harbor at Ostia, just south of Rome at the mouth of the Tiber River, and he restored several major aqueducts that brought water to Rome.

Expanding the empire

Claudius believed in expanding the empire if possible, and he did incorporate three new client kingdoms: Mauretania in 42 CE, Lycia in 43 CE, and Thrace in 46 CE. However, his greatest overseas accomplishment was the annexation of Britain in 43 CE. Claudius himself led the campaign, to make up for his previous lack of military achievement, and it was spectacularly successful. After landing in Kent and defeating the local chieftain Caractacus, the Roman army captured his capital, Camulodunum (present-day Colchester), and established a Roman

from his own household and employed slaves and freedmen as his secretaries and as heads of various departments. Several of these men became very powerful, such as Narcissus, his chief secretary, and Pallas, his chief accountant. Free slaves such as these often abused their positions, however, becoming insolent and greedy. Rome's nobles resented the fact that they had nowhere near as much power as these upstarts.

Claudius and the senate

Claudius himself showed great respect for the aristocracy and the senate, according that body much the same role colony there. Within a year, Claudius returned to Rome, where he was given a triumphal victory procession. His generals remained in Britain to complete the subjugation of the island.

Messalina and Agrippina

In spite of his achievements, Claudius was widely unpopular. His wives were partly responsible. He was married four times, his last two wives being Messalina and Agrippina. Messalina was, according to contemporaries, an unfaithful wife. Young and beautiful, she was said to be discontented with her handicapped *princeps* and would call on young aristocrats from all over the city to spend the night with her, punishing with death any who

refused. Eventually, she began an affair with Gaius Silius. One night in 48 CE, the two of them held a wild party when they believed that Claudius was out of the city. However, Claudius surprised them in the middle of the orgy and found his wife dancing clad only in a leopard skin. Claudius had her locked away for the remainder of the night. The next morning, he seemed ready to pardon her, but before he could do so, Narcissus arranged for her execution together with Silius.

Claudius married again the following year. His new wife, the beautiful but devious Agrippina, was Caligula's sister, the great-granddaughter of Augustus, and Claudius's own niece. She was also

The Apotheosis of Claudius *is a cameo made of sardonyx set in an enameled gold frame. It shows the emperor being taken to heaven by an eagle and marks his deification after his death in 54 CE.*

91

CLAUDIUS THE SCHOLAR

Because of his disabilities, Claudius was largely ignored by the imperial family during his early years, and he lived a quiet and scholarly life. While Claudius was still a young man, the historian Livy encouraged him to study history. Livy's advice resulted in an enormous output; Claudius wrote 20 books on Etruscan history and 8 on Carthaginian history, all in Greek. Claudius also produced a pamphlet in defense of the republican orator Cicero, which sparked an interest in contemporary Roman history. Claudius went on to describe the reign of Augustus in 41 books. In addition to his historical works, Claudius produced an autobiography and a pamphlet on gambling with dice, a pastime of which he was very fond. He made a historical study of the Roman alphabet and even introduced three new characters to it—although they later fell out of use. Highly intelligent, Claudius also taught himself the basics of architecture, which makes it somewhat surprising that he undertook relatively little building work in Rome when he later became emperor. The quality of Claudius's writings is unknown; none of his literary works survived.

the ex-wife of Domitius Ahenobarbus, by whom she had had a son in 37 CE. This son was now 11 years old, and it was Agrippina's ambition to make him *princeps* and then rule through him. Two people stood in the way: Claudius himself and his son Britannicus (named for Claudius's conquest of Britain). In 50 CE, Agrippina used her influence with Claudius to get him to adopt her son, who then took the name Nero. Four years later, in 54 CE, Claudius died suddenly. Rumors claimed that Agrippina had poisoned him with a plate of mushrooms. Afranius Burrus, the commander of the Praetorian Guard, was already under Agrippina's protection, and he declared Nero to be the new *princeps*.

Nero

In 54 CE, when Nero was declared *princeps*, he was just 16 years old and too young to rule. Effective power passed to his regents: the elderly Stoic philosopher Seneca and the commander of the

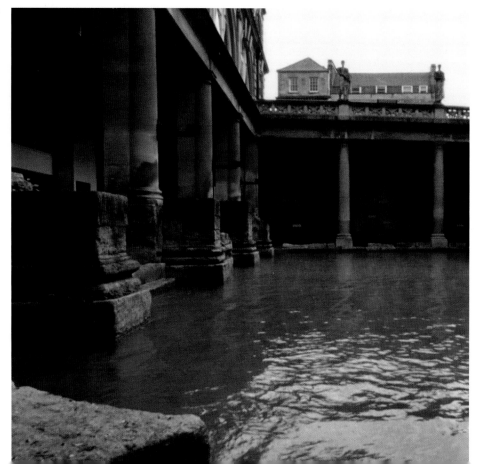

After his conquest of Britain, Claudius built baths at Aquae Sulis (now Bath), using natural hot springs that were already renowned for their curative powers. The emperor's baths were based on a scaled-down version of the great baths in Rome.

Praetorian Guard, Burrus. Burrus and Seneca ruled in an autocratic manner, permitting little if any dissent, but the empire prospered under them. They had inherited a well-ordered empire from Claudius, who had reorganized imperial finances so that taxes from all the provinces were controlled centrally in Rome. (One of the earliest acts of Nero's reign was to deify Claudius.) The state coffers were well filled, and all over the empire, new colonies were being founded, which brought in new revenue.

The young *princeps* had little choice but to allow his mentors to have their own way. In any case, he was less interested in politics and more in the arts; he thought of himself primarily as a poet and singer. Nero's mother, Agrippina, found the situation deeply frustrating. She wanted to rule herself, through Nero, but that was not possible without her son's support.

However, within five years, Nero had turned into a monster. He was to murder, eventually, his stepbrother, his mother, his first and second wives, and his tutor, plus many others.

Murders and marriages

Agrippina fought to keep her influence over her son. According to a story related by the historian Tacitus, Agrippina went so far as to try to seduce Nero during an orgy. Seneca, witnessing her behavior, hastily sent in a beautiful freedwoman called Acte to divert Nero's attention. Realizing that she was losing her influence over her son, Agrippina began to favor Britannicus, Nero's younger stepbrother. Nero promptly had him poisoned.

By 59 CE, Nero had decided to get rid of his interfering mother. He invited

her to one of his country houses, supposedly for a reconciliation. The house was on a lake, so he sent a boat to transport her. The boat was rigged to fall apart in the middle of the lake so that Agrippina would drown. When she managed to swim ashore, Nero abandoned subtlety. He ordered a company of the Praetorian Guards to stab his mother to death. Burrus circulated a rumor that Agrippina had conspired against Nero, and Seneca wrote a statement for Nero to read to the senate to justify her death.

The young emperor rapidly developed into a vicious and pleasure-seeking despot. His behavior was encouraged by his mistress Poppaea Sabina, the wife of

Agrippina originally had considerable influence over her son while she acted as regent, but she later quarreled with him, mainly over his affair with Poppaea Sabina.

ROMANS AND LIFE AFTER DEATH

Although the Romans had largely adopted the Greek mythology and pantheon of gods, they continued to hold on to their own ideas about the afterlife. They believed that besides the soul (or anima, literally meaning "breath" or "wind") something else remained after death, namely the umbra (or shadow). These shadows of the dead made up the large swarms of manes (a word always used in the plural). The manes were able to assist their families by appearing to them in dreams and revelations to offer advice, but manes could also turn against them. Those who offended the manes, by trying to control them with magic potions, for example, would end up having to deal with evil, rather than benign, spirits.

The shadows departed this world into the underworld though cracks in the earth. There, they were transported by the ferryman Charon across the Styx River (the river of the dead) in a boat to the other side, where they were subjected to the decision of two infallible judges.

The condemned ones were thrown into Tartarus, the lowest region of the underworld, to suffer eternal punishment. One such punishment in mythology was meted out to Tantalus, who was forced to stand in water up to his neck while a branch bearing delicious fruit dangled in front of his face. When he wanted to take a drink, the water level would drop out of reach, and when he tried to eat some fruit, the branch would be blown away by the wind.

The saved ones, however, were allowed to enter the Elysian Fields, with their blossoming valleys and multicolored light. The poet Ovid claimed that the blessed replicated their earthly ways of life there, while the poet Virgil told of the shadows of blessed ones who found entertainment there by singing and holding chariot races.

This 16th-century-CE painting by the Flemish artist Joachim Patinier depicts Charon ferrying the dead across the Styx River.

This gold coin from around 55 CE depicts Nero and his mother, Agrippina.

was indeed a talented singer and poet. Nero even went so far as to appear on stage in public. Naturally, the audience was obliged to applaud him enthusiastically.

From a modern perspective, it is impossible to know whether or not Nero actually had any talent. According to historians of the time, including Tacitus, the emperor made a fool of himself. His performances, they said, brought disgrace upon his family and the whole of the Roman aristocracy. In 66 CE, Nero undertook an extended tour of Greece, participating in all the local festivals. At each festival, he was, naturally enough, awarded the prize. The emperor also entered the chariot race at the Olympic Games at Delphi. He drove a chariot so wide that no other competitor could get on the track with him. As a result, he was awarded the victor's crown of laurel leaves.

the senator Marcus Salvio Otho (who later was to be briefly emperor), and Nero's friend Tigellinus, one of the Praetorian Guards. In 62 CE, Nero divorced and murdered his first wife, Octavia, who was a daughter of Claudius. He then married the divorced Poppaea, but in 65 CE, in a wild fit of temper, he kicked her to death. He then married the recently widowed Statilia Messalina (whose husband was also thought to have died at the hands of the emperor).

The "artist"

Burrus died in 62 CE, and Seneca, fearing for his own safety, retired from Nero's court. Nero's attention then focused on Tigellinus, who replaced Burrus as head of the Praetorian Guard. Tigellinus's flattery convinced Nero that the emperor

The fire of Rome

In 64 CE, a fire broke out in Rome. Such fires were a regular occurrence in the huge city, with its maze of narrow streets lined with timber buildings, but the fires were usually put out before much damage was done. This time, however, the fire took hold, and a wall of flame and smoke swept through the alleyways for days, destroying the homes of the poor and claiming thousands of lives. Most of the city was destroyed.

A rumor began that Nero himself started the fire, even though he had been in Antium, which was 35 miles (56 km) from Rome. Another version of the story claimed that Nero stood on a hill, watched the flames devour the city, and sang a song he had written about the fall of Troy. This account was the origin of the modern story that the emperor played the fiddle while Rome burned.

Nero, in return, put the blame for the fire on Rome's Christians (see box, page 98). He initiated a full-scale persecution of thousands of Christians, many of whom were gruesomely put to death during the games in the amphitheater. Others were covered in pitch and used as human torches during the emperor's parties. Such cruelty made many people sympathetic to the Christians, and the rumor that Nero himself started the fire refused to die.

After the fire, Nero decided to rebuild Rome and make it more magnificent than ever. The city was laid out with wider streets on a regular grid pattern. Strict building regulations ensured that all structures were built solidly of fireproof materials. Nero reserved for himself a large tract of land in the eastern part of the city and began to build a new palace, called the Golden House. This sumptuous residence, with colonnades, parks, and lakes, was decorated with magnificent frescoes, which later influenced the work of Renaissance artists. The palace was never finished, however, due to Nero's chronic shortage of money.

Rebellion in Britain

The citizens of the provinces deeply resented the corruption and cruelty of Nero's administrators, and this was particularly true in Britain. In 60 CE, the resentment flared into open rebellion, led by Boudicca, queen of the Iceni tribe in what is now southeastern England. The insurgents took the Roman settlements of Camulodunum (present-day Colchester), Verulamium (St. Albans), and

Londinium (London) and razed them. According to Roman sources, the rebels massacred the settlements' inhabitants, although some modern archaeologists dispute the claim. It was a year before Roman legions regained control, putting Boudicca to death and taking reprisals against the Iceni.

Rebellion at home

In Rome, Nero's poor administration and the growing insecurity he provoked among senators fostered a mood of rebellion. Forty-one prominent Romans hatched a plot to make Gaius Calpurnius Piso emperor, but Nero was warned of the conspiracy by loyal slaves. In 65 CE, Piso and his fellow conspirators were condemned to death. Preferring to take their own lives rather than face the executioners, 18 of the condemned men slit their own wrists. Among them was Nero's former tutor, Seneca. Another one was the general Corbulo, who had been

waging for four years a successful military campaign in Anatolia (modern Turkey) to establish Armenia as a buffer state against Parthia.

Rebellion across the empire

Roman brutality fomented a Jewish revolution in Judaea in 66 CE. An initial rising in Jerusalem was followed by disorder spreading throughout the country. Nero sent Titus Flavius Vespasianus (who eventually became the emperor Vespasian) to end the revolt. Completing a bloody campaign in which he suppressed the rebels village by village, Vespasian began a siege of Jerusalem.

Before the situation in Judaea could be resolved, two provincial governors rebelled in the west: Julius Vindex in Gaul and Sulpicius Galba in Spain. In 68 CE, Roman legions on the banks of the Rhine River slaughtered the Gauls in Vindex's army and forced him to commit suicide. The victorious Roman gen-

The Venetian Renaissance artist Luca Giordano painted **The Death of Seneca** *in 1680 CE. According to the historian Tacitus, Seneca died slowly after cutting his wrists.*

THE CHRISTIANS IN ROME

By the time Nero came to power, a new religious sect had appeared in Rome. The sect had originated in Palestine, where its members worshipped a single god, rather than the multiplicity of Roman deities. The people were known as Christians, after the founder of the sect, Jesus Christ, who had been put to death during the reign of Tiberius. It was said that the Christians expected the imminent return of Christ to punish a world that they believed was full of sin.

Many Romans paid little attention to Christianity. It was just one of a number of eastern sects in Rome, some of which had attracted much controversy. There were rumors, for example, that Christian worship included witchcraft and cannibalism.

Many early Christians in Rome were citizens, who enjoyed the protection of the law. When Paul the Apostle was flogged, for example, and claimed his rights as a citizen, the city council apologized; it was not permitted to flog a Roman. However, noncitizens could be subject to arbitrary martial law. The provincial governor could condemn them to death, as Pontius Pilate did with Jesus.

Paul was arrested and sent to Rome for execution around 62 CE. According to tradition, he was beheaded with a sword, which was his right as a Roman citizen. The apostle Peter was also martyred during the reign of Nero. Because he was not a citizen, however, Peter was crucified, which was more painful. Despite the deaths of these leaders, the sect was not destroyed. Various sources indicate that Christianity became one of the most successful sects in Rome.

This 19th-century-CE sculpture depicts the British queen Boudicca, who led a rebellion against the Romans in the first century CE.

eral claimed that he was acting on behalf of the senate rather than Nero. Meanwhile, Galba and his legions advanced toward Rome unopposed.

The senate condemned Nero to death, and on June 9, 68 CE, having lost the allegiance of the Praetorian Guard, Nero fled the city. A slave helped him stab himself in the throat. The dying emperor was said to have remarked, "What a great artist dies with me!"

Nero's reputation

Nero's death brought an inglorious end to the Julio-Claudian dynasty. Declared *damnatio memoriae* (damned in memory) by the senate, Nero and his reign were obliterated from the official record. Later, under the emperor Domitian, even inscriptions on buildings that referred to Nero were erased.

Nero's historical reputation, however, has undergone something of a rehabilitation. Historians who lived during his reign and in its aftermath agreed with the senators and condemned Nero's tyranny. Modern historians, on the other hand, point out that the emperor actually seems to have been quite popular with ordinary Romans.

It may be that what Rome's leading citizens regarded as tyranny was seen by commoners in a more favorable light—perhaps as an effective means of civic control. While there is no doubt that Nero was highly unpopular in the provinces, which he exploited to the benefit of Rome, the average Roman seems to have had more positive feelings about Nero's time as *princeps*.

The tyrannical behavior of Nero had rarely affected the inhabitants of the alleyways of Rome. Those Romans may have approved—if they noticed—that powerful and corrupt men were being disposed of by the hundreds. What was more, Nero had spent vast sums—more than any other *princeps*—on *panem et*

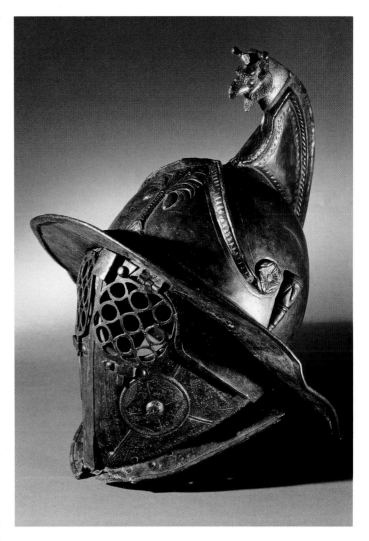

circenses (bread and circuses), the traditional entertainments that the emperors used to keep the masses happy.

Such generosity seems to have been effective. Contemporary records relate that, when the news of Nero's death was heard, all Rome mourned and storekeepers closed their stores. For years afterward, fresh flowers were placed on the burial mound that the freedwoman Acte erected for her imperial lover.

This bronze gladiator's helmet was found at Pompeii and dates to the first century CE.

See also:

The Age of Augustus (page 72) • Daily Life in Rome (page 116) • Expanding the Empire (page 100)

EXPANDING THE EMPIRE

The emperors who came after Nero brought the empire to its greatest extent through a combination of military organization and smart political maneuvers. Even at its most powerful, however, Rome contained signs of its eventual destruction.

After the death of Nero in 68 CE, the senate declared Sulpicius Galba *princeps*. He was a member of a distinguished patrician family and a former governor of Spain, and as such, he was welcomed by the senators as their new emperor. However, Galba's appointment marked a significant departure from the principle of hereditary succession. The new emperor had no connection with the Julio-Claudian dynasty. If he could become emperor (and at the age of 73), then in theory, any member of the aristocracy had a right to the imperial throne.

Galba and Otho

Galba faced a potentially dangerous situation. Law and order broke down in Rome, and for the first time in a century, there was fighting in the streets, with frequent murders and robberies. Nero had virtually emptied the treasury, and the harsh economies Galba introduced made him highly unpopular. Worse still, the legions in the provinces were at war with one another, each supporting its own candidate for *princeps*. The legions in the north, which had been instrumental in engineering Nero's downfall, were particularly bitter. It seemed that their efforts had brought to power someone with whom they had no connection.

In January of 69 CE, shortly after being recognized as *princeps*, Galba learned that the northern legions were in revolt. Under Aulus Vitellius, the commander of Lower Germany, they were preparing to march on Rome. Galba appointed a young, inexperienced patrician named Piso Licinianus to fight the rebellion—and to be his successor. The emperor's decision alienated Marcus Salvius Otho (the first husband of Poppaea Sabina and a confidant of Galba), who had hoped to succeed Galba. Otho, who was a prominent banker, bribed the Praetorian Guard to murder the new emperor in the street.

The senate recognized Otho as emperor. His reign lasted only three months, however. The empire was still in turmoil. The German legions were still advancing on Rome with Vitellius at their head. Otho assembled a hastily formed army and, together with the Praetorian Guard, faced the Vitellian forces at Cremona in northern Italy. Otho's army was defeated, and Otho committed suicide.

Vitellius

Vitellius and his Rhineland army entered Rome in April of 69 CE. The senate confirmed Vitellius as emperor, but this *princeps* lasted only slightly longer than his predecessors: eight months. The problems that confronted his predecessors had not gone away; indeed, the problems had become worse. The treasury's coffers were completely exhausted. Unable to pay his troops their victory bonus, Vitellius lost all control of his army. To make matters worse, Vitellius also came under threat from another pretender to the principate.

It was not only the legions on the Rhine who had wanted to see one of their own become *princeps*. The legions in Judaea had the same idea. There, Vespasian commanded a huge army that had been assembled in Jerusalem to suppress the great Jewish rebellion of 66 CE. Those soldiers nominated Vespasian as *princeps*, and he quickly gained support throughout the region and from the legions along the Danube. In December of 69 CE, Vespasian's army met Vitellius's Rhineland troops at the Battle of Bedriacum, in the northern Italian Peninsula, and defeated them. Vitellius was lynched by the victors.

Vespasian

After the defeat of Vitellius, the senate gave Vespasian the title the legions had demanded for him. The first of the Flavian emperors, Titus Flavius Vespasianus was not a descendant of the old Roman aristocracy. Born in a small Italian town, he did not even come from Rome, and his family had only recently been promoted to the senatorial order. Yet this "outsider" took control of the empire with a firm hand.

Vespasian's rule was authoritarian, but by retaining strict control of the army, he succeeded in bringing much needed peace to the battle-bruised empire. He quickly eliminated all political opponents, banishing them from the capital. He revived and occupied the position of censor, packing the senate with his supporters and greatly increasing the

This marble statue of the emperor Hadrian was carved in the second century CE to celebrate his victories over the barbarians.

101

THE ROMAN EMPIRE AT ITS GREATEST EXTENT

KEY

Roman Empire in 117 CE

✗ Major battle

number of senators drawn from the provinces. Although he allowed the senate little real power, he appointed a large number of senators to administrative positions. During his reign, a new aristocracy, based on government service, became influential.

Vespasian was the first emperor to tackle successfully the financial and organizational chaos left by Nero. Vespasian solved Rome's financial problems by cutting back drastically on state spending and by increasing taxes. He imposed a poll tax on Jews and even taxed the contents of public urinals, which leatherworkers used to tan their hides. When a delegation went to the emperor to ask him to lift the tax, Vespasian held up a coin in front of their noses and asked, "Does this stink?"

In spite of his cutbacks, Vespasian was also careful to build something that would please and entertain Rome's citizens. On the site of Nero's Golden House, Vespasian began building a huge amphitheater, later known as the Colosseum, where contests with wild animals, gladiator fights, and mock naval battles could be staged.

However, serious problems remained in the provinces. The Danube lands were being raided by Saratian tribesmen, but Vespasian's generals were able to restore order there relatively quickly. Along the Rhine in Lower Germany, the trouble was more serious. The fiercely independent Batavian tribe had previously formed an alliance with the Romans and supplied auxiliary troops to the Roman army. Now, the Batavian tribesmen felt increasingly embittered at the authoritarian way in which they believed they were being treated. In the chaotic year of 69 CE, they rebelled, under the leadership of Julius Civilis, a German with Roman citizenship. The rebellion lasted for a year before a settlement was negotiated.

In 70 CE, Vespasian's elder son, Titus, took Jerusalem for his father, finally ending the long war in Judaea. Titus then killed most of the city's inhabitants and destroyed the temple, except for one part of the Western Wall. Known today as the Wailing Wall, it is one of the most holy places of Judaism.

Vespasian's rule lasted for ten years, during which time he carefully groomed Titus to succeed him. When the emperor sensed that his death was near, he is alleged to have said, "Oh dear, I think I'm turning into a god." Titus succeeded his father without problem and promptly had him deified.

Titus

Titus, who was 39 years old on his accession, had intelligence, good looks, and a pleasant personality, but he lived for only two years after becoming emperor. His short reign was dominated by two catastrophes: the eruption of the volcano Mount Vesuvius in 79 CE, which buried the towns of Pompeii, Herculaneum, and Stabiae (see box, page 104), and a major fire in Rome. After both disasters, Titus made considerable efforts to help the survivors, including making donations from his own funds.

Titus also completed the great amphitheater begun by his father and celebrated its opening with games that lasted for more than three months. His generosity and just government made Titus a popular *princeps*, and he was deified after his sudden death at age 41.

Titus was succeeded by his brother Domitian, who may have had a hand in the death and whose name was to become synonymous with terror.

Domitian

The last of the Flavian emperors, Domitian was the second son of Vespasian and had never been designated as heir apparent. Nevertheless, after the death of Titus, Domitian was hailed as the new emperor by the Praetorian Guard and then ratified by the senate. Domitian had never before held a position of influence because his father and elder brother both believed that his ambition made him dangerous. Suddenly, Domitian had complete power, and he used it to instigate a reign of terror.

Treating the senate with contempt, Domitian manipulated it to a greater extent than any previous emperor had.

This coin was minted during the short reign of Sulpicius Galba, who died in 69 CE, only a year after gaining the imperial throne.

He also insisted that the senators pay him the respect he felt he merited, and he meted out severe punishment for any insult, real or imagined. Domitian maintained his control over the senate by appointing senators of his own choice and, later, by executing any of whom he disapproved. In 85 CE, Domitian appointed himself *census perpetuus* (perpetual censor) and repeatedly managed to get himself elected consul, the civilian head of government. While he was willing to alienate the senate, however, Domitian was also shrewd enough to make sure that he kept the allegiance of the army.

Domitian's administration was highly efficient. To administer the provinces, he sent competent, incorruptible men chosen from the senate or the *equites*. The provinces thrived under his authoritarian rule. Believing that his position depended on the goodwill of the masses, he made sure to entertain them with spectacular events, including numerous games in the amphitheater and two triumphal processions through the center of

Otho's reign lasted only three months, from January 15 to April 16, 69 CE.

POMPEII

In 79 CE, Mount Vesuvius, the volcano near Naples that had been dormant for centuries, suddenly erupted, burying the nearby towns of Pompeii and Herculaneum under 13 feet (4 m) of lava and hot ash. The event was described in detail by the Roman writer Pliny the Younger, in an account of the death of his uncle, Pliny the Elder, who was the commander of a naval squadron at the time of the eruption.

"Even though the mountain smoked ominously for a time, the inhabitants of the little towns on the slopes were barely concerned," he wrote. "They were pretty sure that the volcano was extinct.... One afternoon Pliny [the Elder] saw from his ship how the top of the mountain, as it were, exploded. Large gas clouds rose up from the crater. In Pompeii, it rained pieces of stone, the earth trembled and a large stream of lava started to crawl slowly down the mountain. Pliny went ashore to observe the phenomenon close up, but lost his life in doing so."

The report of Pliny the Younger goes on to describe how panic broke out when the people realized too late what was happening and tried to find safe shelter. In the space of a few days, the towns of Pompeii, Herculaneum, and Stabiae disappeared from the face of the earth, covered in lava and ash, together with many of their inhabitants.

It was not until 1748 CE that Pompeii was discovered again. Under the lava, ash, and mud, archaeologists found an entire city, with streets, shops, houses, a forum, several temples, and a large amphitheater. On a more macabre note, it was found that the volcanic debris had formed perfect molds around the bodies of the terrified townspeople. Archaeologists were able to pour plaster into these molds to create perfect replicas of the long-dead people, even reproducing the look of horror on their faces. The excavated Pompeii provides a wealth of information about daily life in a Roman city.

Rome to honor his army's success against tribes in the northeast.

Troubled divinity

From the beginning of his reign, Domitian insisted that he was divine and that people should address him as *dominus et deus* (lord and god). However, he did not at first feel the need to demonstrate the godlike control over human life that he later exhibited. That changed in 89 CE, when Saturninus, the Roman commander on the Rhine, initiated a rebellion by declaring himself *princeps*. The emperor swiftly crushed the revolt in a bloodbath.

After the uprising, Domitian trusted no one. He kept *delatores* (informers) busy looking for conspiracies, and in the senatorial order, nobody's life was safe. Anyone voicing opposition to the emperor was summarily executed. Domitian himself became paranoid, fearing attack even in the safety of his own palace. It was said that he put up mirrors in every room so he could always see who was behind him.

Even the emperor's mirrors could not protect him, however. In 96 CE, he became the victim of the conspiracy he had always feared. Domitian's wife paid a slave to assassinate him, and the emperor was stabbed to death while he was studying a report on a plot to kill him. After his death, the relieved senate declared him *damnatio memoriae* (damned in memory), and his reign was struck from the record. His name was also removed from all public buildings.

Military accomplishments

Domitian's military accomplishments were unquestionable. Under his rule, the borders of the empire had been strengthened and, in some cases, extended. He had also continued the military reforms initiated by Vespasian. To avoid a repeat of the events of 69 CE, when the Batavian tribe had rebelled in Lower Germany, Vespasian had begun a policy of stationing native auxiliary forces far from their homelands, usually under the command of a Roman officer. Auxiliary forces were increasingly assigned roles similar to those once performed by the regular legions, working in small, highly mobile detachments. The legions themselves, which were based in permanent camps, had grown less mobile. Domitian continued these policies and used native detachments to good effect in Britain, along the Rhine and Danube rivers, and on the eastern frontier.

Under three successive governors between 71 and 84 CE, Rome's frontiers in the half-conquered land of Britain were pushed out into what are now

This fresco from Pompeii shows the goddess Venus fishing. The ruined city is a main source of information about Roman painting.

Wales, northern England, and parts of Scotland. Domitian garrisoned three legions in the extended province.

In 74 CE, Vespasian had taken over territory between the Rhine and the Danube. Domitian built extensive fortifications along the new border. He also turned the military regions of Upper and Lower Germany into regular provinces.

In 85 and 86 CE, the powerful Dacian king Decebalus crossed the Danube, invading Roman territory from the north. Domitian's legions halted the advance of Decebalus in 88 CE, but the next year, needing his troops to put down Saturninus's rebellion, Domitian broke off the conflict and negotiated a treaty under which he paid an annual fee to Decebalus, who in return undertook to protect the lower Danube from barbarian attack.

In the east, Domitian completed the development of miliary roads begun by Vespasian in Anatolia. Domitian also kept Judaea under control by settling permanent legions in the area and reinforced the Roman military presence along the Euphrates River by establishing legionary camps at major crossing points.

Nerva

After the assassination of Domitian in 96 CE, the senate was quick to nominate one of its own as *princeps*. The elderly senator Marcus Cocceius Nerva became the first in a sequence of five rulers who were called the Antonine emperors, after their most outstanding representative, Antoninus Pius.

Nerva was a good administrator whose attempts to solve social problems made him popular with the citizens and senators. However, the army remained loyal to Domitian and insisted that any conspirators implicated in his assassination be executed. Eager to placate the army, and lacking any military prestige himself, Nerva quickly adopted a soldier,

This first-century-CE coin shows the emperor Domitian, during whose reign it was struck. After his death, Domitian was declared damnatio memoriae, *and no further memorials were created.*

rather than a member of his own family, as his heir apparent.

Nerva nominated the Spanish officer Marcus Ulpius Trajanus (Trajan), who commanded the troops in Upper Germany. The action initiated a tradition that the emperor adopt a successor on the basis of ability rather than family ties. The new custom was to provide Rome with what history has termed the "good emperors" for the next century, during which the principate flourished.

Trajan

In 98 CE, only three months after nominating Trajan as his successor, Nerva died. He was accorded the deification now traditional for a fair and reasonable emperor. Trajan was serving in Germany when he became emperor and clearly considered that his nomination by the senate was little more than a formality, as indeed proved to be the case. Trajan saw no need to return to Rome until the following year, when he had completed his mission. His decision was an indication of the importance he attached to his immediate task, his commitment to the provinces, and the fact that he was not impressed by constitutional tradition

Trajan was careful, however, to retain the goodwill of the senate. As a provincial Spaniard, he was popular with the increasingly numerous provincial senators. Meanwhile, his modest demeanor and lack of self-importance also endeared him to the aristocratic senators. Trajan's personality did much to allay the fear of terror and conspiracy that had permeated Domitian's court, and he was recognized throughout Rome as an outstanding ruler with high moral values. Once, when handing a sword to the commander of the Praetorian Guard, he is reported to have said, "Use it against me if I neglect my duty, but use it to defend me if I perform my duty well."

Trajan's government

In spite of his modesty, Trajan could be autocratic. He intervened in the affairs of the senate whenever he felt it necessary, ruling with a group of advisers about whom little is known. He aimed to promote public well-being, and he provided gladiatorial games to entertain Rome's citizens. He also sponsored public works, such as new buildings in Rome and improvements to harbors and roads throughout Italy. The emperor's financial experts, the *curatores*, helped municipal towns and, indeed, two provinces that had gotten into financial difficulties. He also made low-cost loans available to farmers and used the interest to fund a children's charity.

Trajan the soldier

Throughout his life, Trajan remained primarily a soldier. He spent seven of his nineteen years as emperor in military camps and died in an army tent. His military ambition was to extend the frontiers of the empire, and he was brilliantly successful.

One of Trajan's greatest military achievements was on the Danube. The Dacians had established a powerful empire in the Carpathian region under Decebalus. Trajan resented the annual payments Rome made to the Dacians under the terms of Domitian's treaty, in return for their policing efforts against the aggressive Sarmatian tribes. Conflict between Rome and the Dacians flared again in 102–103 CE. In a second hard-fought war in 105–106 CE, Trajan's forces built a massive stone bridge to provide a crossing point over the Danube. Roman legions entered the Dacian capital, and the defeated Decebalus took his own life. All Dacians who refused to surrender were hunted down and killed. Trajan's victory was one of the most devastating campaigns in the history of Rome; it destroyed the Dacians as an ethnic group.

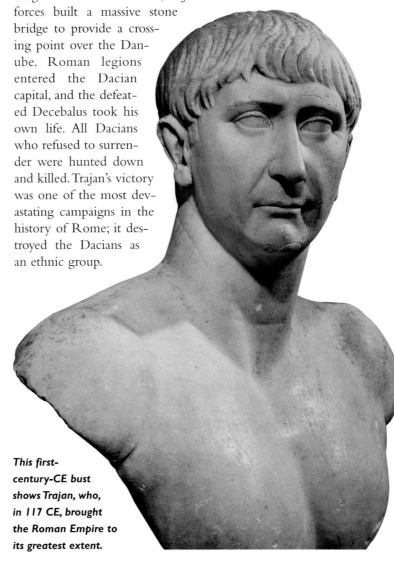

This first-century-CE bust shows Trajan, who, in 117 CE, brought the Roman Empire to its greatest extent.

Trajan's Arch, built in 114 CE by the senate in honor of the emperor, still stands in Benevento in central Italy. The relief carvings on the arch show scenes from the emperor's life and military campaigns.

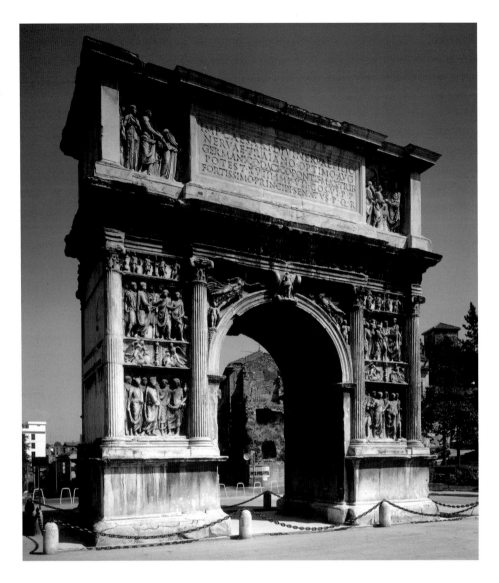

To commemorate his victory, Trajan erected a huge stone column in the new forum he had just completed in Rome. The column was decorated with reliefs showing scenes from the campaign. In the conquered province, the development of a new dialect influenced by Latin was a powerful sign of the obliteration of Dacia. The new language was to become, in time, Romanian.

Trajan continued his conquests, annexing the kingdom of Arabia and the buffer state of Armenia and invading Parthia in 114 CE. By 116 CE, he had conquered Mesopotamia and sailed down the Tigris River to the Persian Gulf. His campaigns had brought the empire to what would be its greatest extent. However, fighting broke out as Jews, Parthians, and other conquered peoples rose in rebellion. Before he could quell these insurrections, Trajan died on campaign in Syria in 117 CE. After his death, he was routinely deified.

Hadrian

Trajan died without nominating an heir. However, his widow claimed that on his

This detail from the reliefs on Trajan's Column shows Roman soldiers being attacked by Dacians in 106 CE.

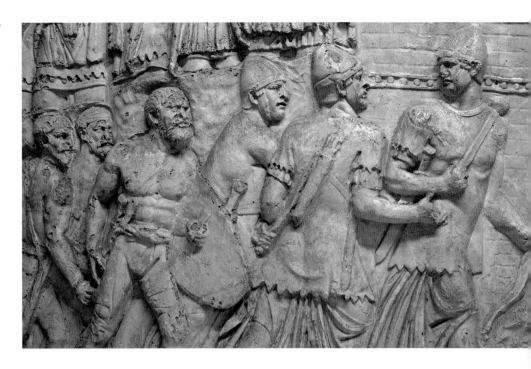

THE JEWISH REBELLIONS

Ever since the Romans had annexed Judaea in 6 CE, they had found the Jews a difficult people to comprehend. They worshipped only one god, of whom they were not allowed to make any statues, and they fanatically refused to worship the Roman emperor as a god. For much of the time, the Romans dealt leniently with the Jews and did not interfere with their religion.

The Jews were divided into two main groups. The Sadducees came from the upper classes and did not take their religion too seriously. The other main group consisted of the Pharisees, who practiced an orthodox form of Judaism and were firmly opposed to Roman rule and influence. The Pharisees were not, however, interested in violent action, unlike the Zealots, who took up arms against the occupying power.

Things came to a head in 66 CE, when the inhabitants of Jerusalem, inflamed by Roman oppression, rose in revolt and massacred the small Roman garrison. The rebellion spread like wildfire throughout Judaea. Vespasian, at that time one of Nero's generals, was dispatched to put an end to the uprising. Before he could do so, political events at home intervened. The insurrection was finally ended by Vespasian's son Titus in 70 CE, when he besieged the city of Jerusalem and reduced it to ruins. Most of the inhabitants were massacred, and those who survived were enslaved.

Some 60 years later, in 131 CE, the Jews rebelled again. This revolt was caused by the emperor Hadrian's misguided attempt to assimilate the Jews into Roman culture. The Jews took up arms under Bar Kochba, and the ensuing war lasted for three years. The Romans eventually put down the insurrection with great ferocity. When order was finally restored, the survivors were scattered throughout the empire. Judaea lost its name and was henceforth called Syria Palestina.

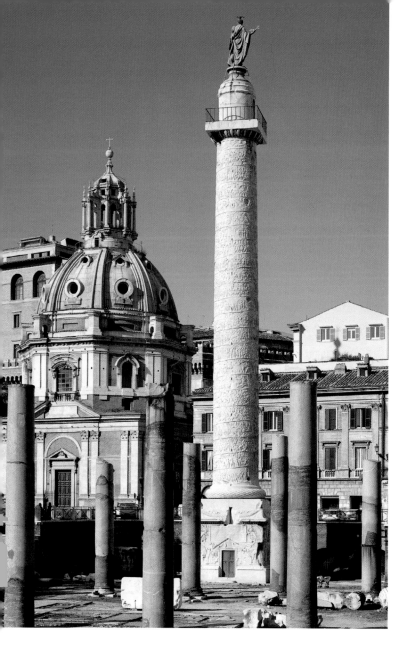

Trajan's Column rises 100 feet (30.5 m) above the ruins of Trajan's Forum in Rome. The column features a spiral band of reliefs illustrating scenes from the emperor's campaign against the Dacians.

excellent administrator. He abandoned his predecessor's aggressive territorial policies and renounced the regions that Trajan had recently conquered in the east. Instead of attempting to expand the empire, Hadrian implemented a policy of protecting its existing frontiers, which made for a more peaceful regime.

Hadrian set up strong fortifications to defend the borders of the empire. The most famous example was Hadrian's Wall in Britain. The tall stone wall, much of which still stands, ran along the top of a mound protected by a ditch and incorporated forts at regular intervals. The wall stretched right across northern Britain and cut off the Picts of Scotland from Roman territory to the south. Hadrian built a similar fortified border between Germany and Raetia.

The only heavy fighting during Hadrian's reign came in Judaea. When the emperor founded a Roman colony in Jerusalem in 131 CE, the outraged Jews rebelled under their leader Bar Kochba. A war followed that lasted until 134 CE (see box, page 109).

Service under Hadrian

To ensure the empire was adequately garrisoned, Hadrian kept his legions and auxiliaries at full strength. He recruited local troops, in contrast to Vespasian's practice of moving auxiliaries away from their homelands. The distinction between auxiliary and legionnaire became blurred, as auxiliaries were increasingly assimilated into the legions. The army also became less influenced by class. Officers were sometimes appointed from the *equites* class rather than, as before, only from the senatorial class. To keep the army in a state of readiness, Hadrian toured the empire to inspect the legions and introduced new field exercises to improve maneuvers. He visited all the provinces and virtually every city, often

deathbed he had adopted Publius Aelius Hadrianus, his closest male relative and the governor of Syria. Mainly on the strength of this claim, Trajan's soldiers nominated Hadrian, another nonaristocratic Spaniard, as the new emperor. Hadrian informed the senate of this decision but did not seek to have his nomination endorsed. His lack of concern about the senate was an indication of how weak it had become.

Hadrian was a civilian rather than a soldier and is best remembered as an making suggestions about how things might be improved.

Hadrian also employed many *equites* in the imperial administration. He abolished the requirement that they perform military service, making it possible for them to follow civilian careers as bureaucrats. *Equites* began to replace freedmen in posts in the imperial household and even appeared on the emperor's advisory council. This encroachment on functions traditionally reserved for members of the senatorial class, coupled with the fact that Hadrian gave the senate no say in the affairs of state, was deeply resented by the senate and cost him much support.

Hadrian's private life

In his private life, Hadrian dabbled in astrology and wrote poetry; his practice of not shaving made beards a new fashion in Rome. He had an enormous villa built for himself at Tivoli, just outside Rome, which broke all the architectural rules of the time. On his travels, he became enamored of a young man named Antinous. Together they took a trip down the Nile, where the youth fell overboard and drowned. The grief-stricken emperor had Antinous deified and, as a memorial, founded a city in Egypt named Antinoupolis.

Hadrian suffered from dark moods in his later years, plagued by ill health and frustrated by his search for a suitable heir. Having executed his young grandson in 136 CE, on suspicion of being involved in a plot, Hadrian had no other male relative. He had adopted Lucius Ceonius Commodus, a man in his 30s with a profligate lifestyle, but Ceonius died soon after. Hadrian, close to death himself, adopted the senator Titus Aelius Antoninus in 138 CE. At the same time, Hadrian stipulated that Antoninus in turn adopt the 18-year-old Marcus Aurelius (nephew of Antoninus's wife) and Lucius Verus (son of Ceonius).

Antoninus Pius

Antoninus was 51 years old when he succeeded. One of Hadrian's reasons for

Hadrian's Wall stretched 73 miles (117.5 km) across northern Britain, with forts at regular intervals for the Roman garrisons.

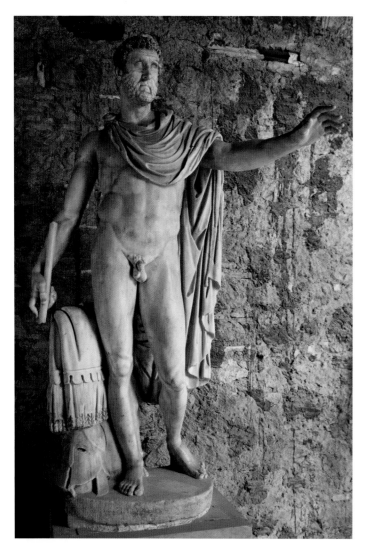

This statue of Antoninus Pius, created in the second century CE, shows the emperor making a gesture of allocution, as if he were making a formal speech.

of his reign, Antoninus remained in Rome, unlike Hadrian. Also unlike his predecessor, Antoninus maintained good relations with the senate. In 148 CE, he ordered spectacular celebrations to mark the 900th anniversary of the traditional founding of Rome.

Antoninus was deified by the Senate on his death in 161 CE. Marcus Aurelius wrote of him: "My predecessor and adoptive father, Antoninus Pius, was a model of simplicity and perseverance, of disdain for hollow words, of diligence and resolve. He … respected the rights of all. I learned from him … to serve humankind unselfishly."

Marcus Aurelius

Marcus Aurelius was just past 40 when he inherited the empire, and he set out to follow his predecessor's example by serving it unselfishly. Although he aimed to rule benignly over a peaceful people, he was forced to spend much of his time on campaign repelling various border incursions. The unhappy but dutiful emperor, who was a follower of Stoic philosophy, asked himself in his *Meditations*: "Are you satisfied, having done what nature demands of you, as if the eye would expect payment for looking and the foot a wage for walking?"

One of Aurelius's first acts as emperor was to make Lucius Verus co-emperor. When the Parthians grew more threatening in the east, Aurelius sent Verus with an army under the command of the Syrian Avidius Cassius to deal with the situation. Cassius, with little help from Verus, secured the imperial borders and client kingdoms in the east by 166 CE.

When the army returned to Rome, however, it brought the plague with it. The disease then raged unchecked throughout the empire for years. The epidemic greatly sapped Roman morale. Among other signs of a growing weakness at the heart of the empire were

nominating him was the expectation that the senator would soon die, leaving the throne open for Marcus Aurelius. In fact, Antoninus lived another 23 years. He persuaded the senate (with some difficulty) to deify Hadrian, and his efforts are said to have earned him the name Antoninus Pius (Antoninus the Pious).

Antoninus's peaceful reign was disturbed only by occasional border raids. The emperor's only exercises in territorial expansion were to advance the empire's frontiers in Britain (where the Antonine Wall marked the new boundary), Dacia, and the Rhineland. For most

In this carving created around 180 CE in Rome, defeated barbarians beg for mercy from the emperor Marcus Aurelius.

recurring incursions by migrating Germanic peoples along the frontiers and even into northern Italy.

Aurelius and Verus managed to fight off the Germans, but in 169 CE, Verus died, possibly of a stroke, leaving Aurelius to finish the campaign. It took Aurelius six more years to push the invaders back across the Danube and restore peace to the region. In 175 CE, Cassius heard a rumor that Aurelius had died. Cassius declared himself emperor in the east. The

This marble bust is a contemporary portrait of Marcus Aurelius.

Government in the provinces

During the first two centuries CE, the Roman Empire enjoyed an unprecedented period of prosperity and peace. Large areas in the west and north were economically developed for the first time, and Roman roads and ports—and Roman garrisons and warships—ensured that trading could take place safely from one end of the Mediterranean to the other.

This large empire was administered by provincial governors, assisted by a retinue of officials. The tasks of the governors included the collection of taxes, the maintenance of law and order, and the administration of justice. In this last capacity, the governors visited all the cities in their provinces to act as judges in trials. A governor was paid a salary, but there were various legitimate ways in which he could supplement his income. If he had been commander of an army, for example, he had the right to confer Roman citizenship—a valuable commodity that was often for sale.

Provincial life

Many of the provincial cities had municipal status, which allowed them virtual self rule. These cities were ruled by a town council of magistrates, elected by the people. The magistrates received no payment for their services. On the contrary, they were expected to give a huge public banquet when they were nominated and to provide charity to the population out of their own pockets. Consequently, they tended to be members of a wealthy aristocracy.

Throughout the provinces, Roman language (Latin) and culture became the

rumor of Aurelius's death was mistaken, but the rebellion Cassius had begun lasted for two years, until he was murdered by his own troops.

While Aurelius's attention was focused on the east, Germanic peoples once more threatened the Danube border. Returning to central Europe, Aurelius barely had time to resecure the border before he died in Vindobona (present-day Vienna) in 180 CE. The empire was left to Aurelius's 19-year-old son, Commodus.

norm. The army played a significant role in the process of Romanizing the empire. Legions were stationed in permanent encampments throughout the provinces to maintain order. The 6,000 or so men who made up each legion lived with their families in simple huts, either inside or near to the camp. After completing a term of 16 years, all legionnaires were entitled to a bounty in the form of either a sum of money or a farm. Many chose the farm and became permanent citizens of the province in which they had served. A large number of them also married local women and started families, becoming assimilated into provincial society.

The legions' camps soon grew into towns, which in turn became centers where farmers and traders from the surrounding area could come to trade their goods. Legionnaires also contributed to the development of a region by building roads and bridges, digging canals, and draining marshes, activities introduced by the emperors to keep the army occupied during times of peace. Such examples of the Roman lifestyle appealed to many people and encouraged immigration into the Roman provinces.

See also:

The Edges of the Empire (page 126) • The Julio-Claudian Emperors (page 84)

A Germanic warrior blows a lur horn during a battle against the Romans. This detail comes from the sarcophagus of the emperor Hostilian, who died in 251 CE.

DAILY LIFE IN ROME

For the poorer citizens, life in ancient Rome could be extremely brutal. To distract the poor from their hardships, Rome's rulers organized lavish entertainments. Among the most popular entertainments were gladiatorial contests and chariot races.

Life in ancient Rome was a lot harsher for some sectors of society than for others. There is no doubt that rich Romans lived a life of luxury in well-built, airy houses that were heated in winter and cool in summer. Rich Romans entertained their friends at dinner parties and soirees and were waited on by slaves. Many rich Romans also had villas in the countryside, so they could escape from the heat of summer.

It was a different story for the city's poorer inhabitants. They were crammed into the working-class residential areas, the narrow, noisome streets which were lined with ramshackle apartment buildings put up by speculators. It was here that the ordinary Roman had his small, dark apartment, separated from his neighbors by the flimsiest of walls. It was not unusual for a building to collapse, and because the Romans used earthenware stoves for cooking and heating and oil lamps for light, fires were a common occurrence. When a fire broke out, the fire brigade (founded by the emperor Augustus) was mobilized, but because water had to be carried by bucket from the Tiber River, it was often impossible to extinguish the fire completely. Instead, the fire would simply be contained until it burned itself out.

In the earliest days of the empire, around a million citizens crowded the narrow streets of Rome by day, which made getting around difficult. The wealthy Romans, carried in sedan chairs, forced their way through the throng. The worst chaos was on the famous Argiletum, where Romans congregated to do their daily shopping. Located between the forum and the Tiber River, there was a large and thriving trading district. All kinds of goods, brought by river from the harbor town of Ostia, were bought and sold. Artisans and craftsmen had their own district, where shoemakers, wool merchants, barbers, smiths, flaxworkers, and others worked side by side. Those people who were engaged in the same trade joined together in a *collegium* (see box, page 118), an early form of a trade guild.

Bread and circuses

The teeming mass of people constituted a potential hotbed of disaffection and disorder, and to appease them, the authorities laid on plenty of entertainment. The poet Juvenal (c. 55–140 CE) said that all that the Roman populace wanted was *panem et circenses* (bread and circuses). For generations, the Roman emperors gave them both. Even in the time of the republic, officials tried to win popularity with grain handouts, enormous spectacles, and huge public sporting events.

The practice of making distributions of grain was made necessary by the fact that the urban poor had very little regular work, owing to the limited opportunities open to them in commerce and industry. The custom took various forms over the centuries. In the second century BCE, the tribune Gaius Gracchus arranged for grain to be sold at fixed low prices. In 60 BCE, Publius Clodius Pulcher organized a system of free handouts. This practice was continued by the emperors as a way of pacifying their poorest subjects.

The grim life of the poor in Rome could also be enlivened by public spectacles, and the typical Roman year offered ample opportunities for celebration. Some of the festivities dated as far back as the time of the kings and were mentioned in the calendar of the legendary King Numa Pompilius. Other festivities had been instituted by the people to appease the gods in difficult times.

The popular *ludi magni* (big games) dated from the year 217 BCE, when the Carthaginian leader Hannibal had threatened Rome's existence. Games

This Roman dice set is made out of bone. Gambling with dice was a popular pastime in ancient Rome.

This relief from a sarcophagus depicts a shoemaker at work.

honoring Caesar and Augustus were instituted by their successors, and in the era of the emperors, new celebrations were added continually. In the second and third centuries CE, the Roman year included almost as many holidays as working days.

Each district had its own guardian spirit, and its altar was the focal point of the annual festivities organized by the local residents in its honor. These festivals grew so out of hand that the state had to create rules to regulate them. The government also had to establish rules for the festivities organized by the *collegia* of the various trades. When these festivities fell too close together, they could cause mayhem. On the ninth of June, for example, the *collegium* of millers and bakers held its celebrations, while on the thirteenth, the *collegium* of musicians held its equivalent. In both festivities, the drunken participants wandered through the streets creating havoc.

COLLEGIA

The *collegium* was an early form of trade guild that functioned primarily as a social club. However, *collegia* also provided other services for their members. For example, records found in Lavinium show that one of the main objects of the Brotherhood of Diana and Antinous was to ensure that its members received a decent burial.

Each member of the brotherhood paid a joining fee of 20 gold pieces and an amphora of good wine. Thereafter, he paid an annual subscription of 3 gold pieces. In return, the brotherhood provided a funeral for 60 gold pieces.

The brotherhood appointed a new chairman every five years. His duties were not onerous. He had to supervise the affairs of the club and organize a meeting of the members six times a year. Every two months, the members met up to attend a drunken feast.

Some brotherhoods also became involved in local politics. Graffiti on a wall in the city of Pompeii reads, "We don't want any Egyptian judges." This message may refer to a brotherhood devoted to the Egyptian goddess Isis, some of whose members had put themselves forward for the city council.

The blood games

Of all the public spectacles, the blood games were the most popular. There were three main types of combat: man to man, in which gladiators fought each other; man to animal, in which wild animals were brought out to fight gladiators; and animal to animal. All these games were held in an amphitheater, in which the audience sat in tiered rows around an arena, where the action took place.

Gladiatorial combat had a religious background. The Etruscan people, who lived on the Italian Peninsula before the Romans, had organized fights to the death between prisoners of war at the funerals of prominent men. The victims were intended as human sacrifices to the dead.

When the Romans adopted this practice around the third century BCE, the fights developed into a bloody spectator sport, a new and extremely popular form of mass entertainment. Schools were founded to train the gladiators, and the games organizers could "order" particular gladiators from these schools for special performances. Originally, the combatants were prisoners of war, convicted criminals, or slaves rented or sold to the schools. Some of the gladiators were volunteers who were seeking excitement and adventure or the riches a successful combatant could gain, despite the fact that most gladiators met a grisly death in the arena.

The audiences enjoyed these exhibitions, eagerly discussing the performances of the combatants and placing bets on their favorites. To add to the spectacle, the gladiators were often dressed in striking costumes, perhaps in an expensive suit of armor or as Neptune with a net and trident. At the end of the fight, the victor would sometimes keep his opponent pinned to the ground while the audience decided the loser's fate, indicat-

ing whether they wanted him to live or die by motioning with their thumbs. It is believed that if the crowd turned their thumbs down, the defeated man would be spared. However, if the audience turned their thumbs up, it was an indication that he should die. The victor received tumultuous applause and was rewarded with a cash prize. Occasionally, after a series of wins, a gladiator might be set free, to live on his earnings for the rest of his life or become a trainer of other gladiators.

The average Roman saw nothing wrong with gladiatorial combat and would even take his children to watch the games, believing that it was a good thing for children to be confronted with violence at an early age. Only a few intellectuals were repelled by these exhibitions, because they found them boring or thought them bad for the soul. Nobody pitied the gladiators themselves, much less the animals.

This mosaic from the second century CE depicts a gladiator killing a panther. Fights between humans and animals were common in Roman arenas.

119

This armor belonged to a type of gladiator known as a secutor. The secutor usually fought against a retiarius, who was armed with a trident and a net.

The games gradually grew bigger and more ambitious. Sometimes, whole battles were staged—even mock naval battles in a flooded arena or on an artificial lake. These mock naval battles and the games involving exotic animals were the most expensive to stage.

Games involving animals took many different forms. There were fights between odd combinations of animals—for example, between a bear and a rhinoceros, or a wild ox and a lion. There were also hunts, where trained hunters downed wild animals with arrows and spears. Animals were also pitted against humans. Some convicted criminals were given wooden sticks to defend themselves. Others were presented to starved beasts of prey completely unarmed, or even tied to a pole. The latter was often the fate of Christians condemned to death by the Roman authorities.

Chariot races

Another popular sport was chariot racing. Every city had its own racetrack, or circus. The Circus Maximus, lying between the Palatine and Aventine hills in Rome, was used from around 600 BCE to the sixth century CE and was famous throughout the empire. At the height of its popularity, in the second century CE, the Circus Maximus could accommodate 250,000 spectators. The arena was 1,850 feet (564 m) long and 280 feet (85 m) wide and was entirely surrounded by three tiers of seats, except for a stall at one end for horses and chariots. A low wall, called the *spina* (spine), ran down the center of the arena, and racing horses and chariots ran around it.

The chariot races were traditionally a religious spectacle, dedicated to the gods. Each race day in Rome started with a solemn procession, in which statues of the gods were carried around the racetrack, while the official who had organized the event dressed up as Jupiter. Each race, in which four or more chariots took part, consisted of seven laps. As many as 24 races could be held in a day. Each driver wore the colors of the circus school or party to which his horses belonged. These colors were originally green, blue, red, and white, but under the later emperors, only green and blue were used. The audience was divided into groups of supporters for each color. Even the emperor picked a team.

The chariots were usually pulled by four horses. The driver, who was generally a young freedman, was strapped to his horses, and if he fell, he had to cut the straps if he was to survive. The chariots often crashed into each other, and injuries and fatal accidents were common. The drivers hung amulets around their necks and on their horses for luck and used incantations to summon demons against their opponents. The emperor was always present at the races, to receive the cheers of the crowd and to show that he enjoyed the same sport as his people.

The theater

During the days of the empire, theaters existed right alongside the circuses and the amphitheaters. Theaters could also accommodate large numbers of people,

This fresco depicts a chariot race. Chariot races were popular forms of entertainment from the early days of the republic onward.

THE BATHS

Roman cities were dirty, dusty, and hot, so, like their Greek equivalents, the Roman authorities built public baths for their citizens. The baths soon developed into community centers, where people met socially, bathed, swam, had massages, or performed gymnastic exercises. There were even opportunities for study, because there was often a well-stocked library in the bath complex.

The baths found at Pompeii, which date from around 75 BCE, included the extensive dressing rooms and the cold, warm, and hot baths that were typical of that era. Far more magnificent were the huge, marble-lined and vaulted Baths of Caracalla, completed in Rome in 216 CE. They could accommodate 1,600 bathers and provided swimming pools, exercise facilities, lounges, and lecture halls.

The Baths of Caracalla, among the largest and most spectacular baths in the Roman Empire, were completed in 216 CE.

but the masses were more interested in the delights of the arena than those of the stage. While Greek theaters had been built into hillsides, Roman theaters were freestanding. The earliest examples were temporary wooden structures; anything more permanent was considered unnecessarily extravagant.

The first permanent Roman theater was built in 55 BCE on the orders of Pompey. To justify the expense of the theater's construction, Pompey erected a temple in the theater and dedicated it to his patron goddess, Venus Victrix. Pompey filled his theater and its gardens with artifacts looted from Greece, creating a monument both to Roman might and to his own achievements.

There was little original Roman writing for the theater. Audiences were more interested in the traditional pieces with which they were familiar. Theatrical performances consisted of endless repeats, which the public watched in order to compare the talents of the actors. To add interest, directors increased the role of the chorus, and the sung text—the *canticum*—began to overshadow the rest of the play. Eventually, the spoken text was abandoned altogether in favor of mime, and the leading actor performed the play without words, to the accompaniment of music and the *canticum*. It was from these origins that opera and ballet later developed.

Another popular form of theater was the tragedy, particularly that of the first-century-CE playwright and Stoic philosopher Seneca. The characters in his plays tended to have introspective natures and to exhibit Stoic fatalism (see box, page 125). His tragedies were written in verse, and the plots were adapted from Greek legends. The plays were revived during the Renaissance and influenced later European drama.

This detail from an actor's sarcophagus depicts two tragic masks.

Wealthy Romans lived in great luxury. This villa at Pompeii once belonged to a successful merchant.

Poetry

The rich and educated Romans spent much of their free time attending recitals of poetry and prose. According to Pliny the Younger, such events could be extremely boring. He recorded that the year 97 CE "brought us a fine crop of poets. During the month of April we had a reading by one or other poet almost every day. Most of the invited guests stay in the foyer, chatting, and only go in toward the end, hoping against hope that the author has finished."

Poetry competitions were held occasionally in Rome and in other cities. The panel of judges usually consisted of priests—not perhaps the best experts to assess poetry. Little is known about any prize-winning poets, but Florus, a poet who published several small works in the time of Hadrian, was once refused a prize. The audience revered him most of all, he recorded, but the emperor did not want to reward Florus because he was not a pure Roman.

Education

Education was generally reserved for the sons of upper-class families. Some sons were sent to school, although Roman schools, often run by discharged soldiers trying to make a living, were not very

STOICISM

Stoicism was the most influential school of philosophy in Rome during the first and second centuries CE. It played a crucial role in the development of the concept of natural law that underlay all Roman legal theory.

The school of Stoicism was founded by the Greek philosopher Zeno of Citium, who lived in the fourth and third centuries BCE. The Stoics were primarily concerned with the study of ethics. They believed that to live in accordance with nature or reason is to live in accordance with the divine order of the universe. Because everything that happens is the result of divine will or, in any case, is outside one's control, a person should calmly accept whatever fate brings, free of all emotions such as passion or grief, or even joy. This calm acceptance constitutes wisdom, one of the four virtues of Stoicism, along with courage, justice, and temperance.

It was perhaps the cosmopolitan nature of Stoicism that made it attractive to the Romans, given their vast empire. Because all beings are seen as manifestations of a single universal spirit, they should live in a state of equality. Race and rank are merely external differences that should be of no importance in genuine social relationships. Among the most important Roman Stoics were the statesman Cato the Younger and the emperor Marcus Aurelius.

impressive. There were few books, and those were very expensive, so most learning was done by rote. Apart from the basic skills of reading and writing, little else was taught.

Wealthy families often engaged an educated slave who was familiar with literature and philosophy to teach their sons. Such teachers were known as pedagogues.

The writings of Virgil, Lucan, and Horace were important texts for pupils in the emperor Vespasian's day, while Greek masters would place great emphasis on Homer and Menander. The study of these great writers was usually as far as education went. However, some older pupils might go on to a school of rhetoric, where they would be taught the art of public speaking, together with some history, which would be useful in political debate.

See also:

The Edges of the Empire (page 126) •
Revolution and Reform (page 44)

This Roman fresco depicts a musician playing a cithara, a musical instrument similar to a lyre.

THE EDGES OF THE EMPIRE

By the early second century CE, the Roman Empire covered the entire Mediterranean world. While some of the peoples who lived outside the boundaries of this area were enemies of Rome, others were valued trading partners.

The Roman Empire reached its greatest extent during the reign of the emperor Trajan, who ruled between 98 and 117 CE. By the time of Trajan's death, the empire stretched from the borders of Scotland in the northwest to the upper Nile in the southeast. While the Romans ruled confidently over the territories they had conquered and annexed, they knew comparatively little about the regions beyond their borders. The little information that did reach the Romans suggested that this hinterland was a hostile and threatening place. The tribes that inhabited the areas around the edges of the empire often harassed the Roman frontier, which had to be permanently garrisoned to keep out the enemy.

Europe

Although a small number of important provinces were added in the years that followed, the broad extent of the Roman Empire had been established by the time of the death of the emperor Augustus in 14 CE. Augustus had suggested that his successors should not attempt to extend the empire further, and the emperors of the first century CE generally followed this advice. In Europe, the Rhine and Danube rivers were regarded as natural boundaries, and the Romans rarely tried to conquer the areas beyond them. Most emperors did not want the financial bur-

den of an expensive military campaign; they were also not keen to allow their generals to gain personal glory from such conquests.

Generally, the Romans had only scant knowledge of the tribes of northern Europe beyond the Roman frontier. One exception to this rule was the Roman historian Tacitus (c. 56–120 CE). Tacitus thought highly of the Germanic tribes and believed they exhibited some of the ancient Roman virtues, such as simplicity of lifestyle, personal fidelity, and great bravery. According to Tacitus, the Germans were as yet unspoiled by the decadence of the civilized world.

Tacitus's view of German life was far removed from reality, however. Most groups lived in great poverty and were constantly involved in local wars. They elected a leader or king only in times of great emergency, when a warrior was lifted on a shield in a meeting of free men. The power of these leaders depended largely on their success in battle. Those who led their people into the rich border territories of the Romans seem to have acquired enormous prestige, eventually making their kingships hereditary.

Hadrian's Wall, built in northern Britain around 122 CE to keep the Picts out of the southern region controlled by the Romans, marked the physical frontier of the empire.

THE ROMAN EMPIRE AND NEIGHBORING PEOPLES

KEY

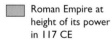 Roman Empire at height of its power in 117 CE

✗ Major battle

The Germanic tribes of central-northern Europe were migrants and had displaced the Celts who had inhabited the territory previously. The Celts were spread all over western Europe, including Gaul and the northern Roman province of Britain. Here, in the extreme north, in a region called Caledonia (present-day Scotland) lived a warlike people known to the Romans as the Picts. Around 122 CE, the emperor Hadrian built a fortified wall across the country to keep the Picts out. However, the Romans never com-pletely managed to stop the Picts from raiding south of the wall.

The eastern border

On its eastern border, the Roman Empire rarely extended beyond the Euphrates River into Mesopotamia. On the other side of the river lay the territory of the Parthians. Divided into small, patriarchal groups, the Parthians had lived for centuries in what is now northeastern Iran. They lived peacefully under the Persian and the early Seleucid kings (see box, page 130) until around 250 BCE, when a neighboring people, the Bactrians, rebelled against their Seleucid overlords. Soon afterward, the Parthian king Arsaces succeeded in gaining independence from the Seleucids and extending his territory to the southwest.

Over the next 200 years, the Parthians profited from the weakening of the Seleucid Empire by increasing their own power. Eventually, the Parthians controlled all of ancient Persia and Mesopotamia. In 63 BCE, when Pompey the Great created the Roman province of Syria out of the remnants of the Seleucid Empire, the Parthians became Rome's neighbors and rivals. They remained so for the next 300 years.

Between 114 and 117 CE, the Roman emperor Trajan mounted a huge expedition to the east and succeeded in conquering the whole of Mesopotamia. In the process, he destroyed the Parthian capital Ctesiphon. Trajan died before he could consolidate his gains, however, and his successor, the emperor Hadrian, gave up Mesopotamia and made peace with the Parthians. Toward the end of the second century CE, the Parthians suffered another heavy defeat at the hands of the Romans, when the emperor Septimius Severus annexed the north of Mesopotamia to the Roman Empire, again reducing Ctesiphon to ruins.

The Parthians never really recovered from these blows, largely due to the weak political organization of their empire. In spirit, they had always remained a nomadic people and did not feel permanently rooted in the lands of Mesopotamia and Persia. Around 230 CE, their empire finally collapsed when Persians from the south rebelled against Parthian rule. The Parthian dynasty was replaced by a new family of Persian rulers, called the Sassanid dynasty. Intent on restoring the old Persian Empire, the Sassanids continued the centuries-old war against Rome with renewed energy, but the decades of strife that followed only led to the chronic weakening of both empires.

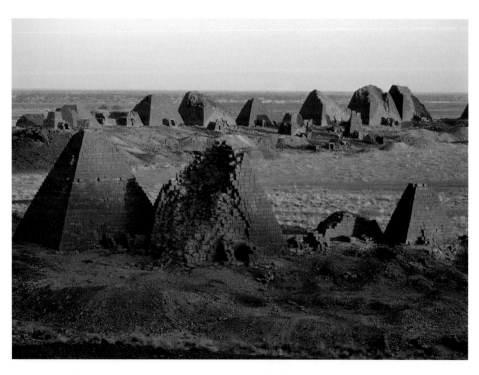

These pyramids are located at Meroë, the ancient capital of Nubia, a kingdom that lay to the south of Egypt.

THE SELEUCIDS

The Seleucid dynasty was founded in the late fourth century CE by Seleucus I, a former general in the army of Alexander the Great. By the time of his death in 281 BCE, Seleucus had succeeded in conquering Anatolia, Babylonia, Assyria, Parthia, Bactria, and a number of other areas of Asia that had formerly been part of the Macedonian Empire. However, over the next half century, the dynasty suffered from constant disputes over the succession, which weakened the empire to such an extent that it lost eastern Iran and the greater part of Anatolia. In 223 BCE, a new, energetic king, Antiochus III, came to the throne. He made determined efforts to recover control of the provinces in the east and to expand his territory in the west. However, when he came up against the power of Rome, he was driven back and defeated in 190 BCE.

Antiochus was succeeded by Seleucus IV, who inherited an empire that stretched from east of the Persian Gulf to Syria and Phoenicia in the west. By 140 BCE, however, the whole region east of Syria had fallen to the Parthians. Pompey's annexation of Syria in 63 BCE brought the Seleucid Empire to an end.

Egypt and Nubia

When Augustus defeated the Egyptian queen Cleopatra at the Battle of Actium in 31 BCE, he moved swiftly to annex the whole of Egypt as a Roman province. By doing so, he inherited the Egyptians' rivalry with the Nubians, a warlike desert people who inhabited part of what is present-day Sudan. The Nubians had been intermittent enemies of the Egyptians for centuries. By Augustus's time, they had become formidable opponents. The Nubian Empire, centered around the city of Meroë, shared many cultural elements with that of the ancient Egyptian pharaohs. At the time of the Roman annexation, the Nubian queen was constantly harassing the Egyptian border, sending warrior bands to raid southern Egypt.

Because Rome depended on grain supplies from Egypt, Augustus sent an expeditionary force to defeat the Nubians. The legions penetrated Nubia almost as far as Meroë. The Romans set up a garrison in the region to maintain

These ruins stand in the city of Ctesiphon, the capital of the Parthian Empire. This palace was built between the third century CE and the sixth century CE by successors of the Parthians.

THE RICHES OF ARABIA

For centuries, the wealthy merchant cities of southern Arabia occupied a pivotal position between the east and the west. The cities' inhabitants owed their prosperity to the trade in Indian spices and their own desert products, such as incense. Particularly prosperous was the city of Aden. Merchants from Egypt and Syria, with whom it traded, called the area around the city "Happy Arabia" because of its extensive irrigation works that allowed it to grow crops in a region that was otherwise covered in desert.

Eventually, in the second century BCE, the Egyptians discovered the secret of the Arabs' maritime trade with India. The monsoon winds blew across the Indian Ocean in one direction for six months of the year and in the reverse direction for the other six months. Ships could take advantage of the change of wind direction and sail back and forth across the vast ocean. Once this secret was out, the inhabitants of southern Arabia lost their monopoly on Indian trade. Southern Arabia retained its importance only as a supplier of incense, which was transported north by caravan via the old trading center of Mecca. As Arabia declined, the irrigation works around Aden fell into disuse. By the Middle Ages, the area was little different from the rest of the barren peninsula.

The Nile River, shown here, flows through Egypt. The province of Egypt marked the southeast boundary of the Roman Empire.

131

FOEDERATI

During the time of the Roman republic, the *foederati* (designated allies) were tribes who were bound by treaty to the Romans yet did not form official Roman colonies. They were allowed to maintain their own institutions and legal and state systems, but they had to supply soldiers for the Roman army on demand.

In the third century CE, the empire was riddled with internal strife, and numerous tribes living on the borders exploited the situation by invading the Roman provinces. Although the invaders were often driven back, the victories were never conclusive. Eventually, the Romans decided to allow the invading tribes to settle in the empire, on the condition that they accepted Roman authority and provided troops to augment the army. This move brought peace to the borders, and the new settlers acted as buffers against future attacks.

control over this southernmost outpost of the empire. Nevertheless, Roman influence in Nubia remained minimal.

Arabia and Africa

At the same time that he mounted the expedition against the Nubians, Augustus sent an army into Arabia. The campaign was a disaster, however. A six-month march through the desert claimed many lives, and the survivors had to turn back before they could achieve their goals.

On the coast of northern Africa, the Romans had conquered and destroyed Carthage in the second century BCE. The lands of the Carthaginian Empire had subsequently been annexed as the Roman province of Africa. Roman power never extended far into the hinterland, however. Like the Carthaginians before them, the Romans were satisfied with the fertile regions on the African coast. The Sahara Desert, just south of the coastal rim, was a formidable barrier that effectively put a stop to any further expansion.

The Romans maintained good relations with the nomadic Berber people who inhabited the region of present-day Morocco and Algeria. Until the third century CE, when unrest spread throughout the empire, there was little to disturb the peaceful life of the Romans living in the rich coastal areas of northern Africa. The many ruins of Roman villas and cities in the region are a testament to its prosperity.

Asia

For several centuries, India was separated from the Roman Empire by the land of the Parthians. Egypt, however, engaged in maritime trade with India from the late second century BCE onward, and once Egypt became a Roman province in 30 BCE, trade between Rome and India grew. Many Roman coins have been found on the coasts of India, suggesting that trading contacts were frequent. India offered spices such as cinnamon and nutmeg, plus pearls, ivory, textiles, and exotic animals. These goods were traded for Alexandrian glass, bronze kitchenware, and minted gold and silver coins. Imports from India were always luxury items, which were eagerly sought after by wealthy, upper-class Roman citizens.

All that the Romans knew about China was that it lay far to the east and produced silk. Toward the end of the second century BCE, the Chinese had established an overland trading route that would carry their silk to the west, where

These Roman ruins stand in the Tunisian city of Dougga. Like much of northern Africa, Dougga was occupied by the Romans in the second century BCE.

it found ready buyers. A stream of merchants with pack animals moved steadily from China to the foot of the Pamir Mountains, where their goods were transferred to the hands of Persian and Syrian merchants, who continued the journey to the west. This was the famous Silk Road, which remained the only regular link between China and the west until the Middle Ages.

See also:

The Age of Augustus (page 72) • The Decline of Rome (page 134) • The Disintegration of the Empire (page 148) • Expanding the Empire (page 100) • The Julio-Claudian Emperors (page 84)

This statue was found in the wreckage of a Roman ship that had sunk off the coast of Tunisia. The ship contained a number of works of art that were being transported to Roman villas in northern Africa.

THE DECLINE OF ROME

The rise of the emperor Commodus to the throne in 180 CE ushered in an unstable period of Roman history. The following century saw a succession of short-reigning emperors, many of whom had to contend with rival claimants.

By the late second century CE, cracks had begun to appear in the Roman Empire. Commerce and industry were in decline, bringing urban decay and political chaos. Agriculture, too, was deteriorating, leading to poverty and unrest in the once-flourishing provinces. Renewed invasions, civil war, and economic ruin would all be factors in the eventual collapse of the empire.

Many of these problems were rooted in the era of the Antonine emperors, although that period itself had seemed to be one of great prosperity. For nearly 100 years, each emperor had nominated a non-relative as his successor. This system had generally proved to be successful. The years of good government ended, however, when Marcus Aurelius nominated his young son, Commodus, to be emperor.

Commodus

Commodus was nominally made co-emperor at age 16. He inherited the empire three and a half years later in 180 CE. Marcus Aurelius's intention had been to train Commodus for the position, but the young man seems to have paid little attention to his lessons. Instead, he was interested only in seeking his own pleasure. Once Commodus inherited the crown, he became extremely paranoid; he lived in constant fear for his life and summarily executed anyone he suspected of plotting against him. He handed out the work of the empire to a collection of his favorites, leaving himself free to enjoy the delights of Rome.

Commodus ignored his father's foreign policy, including plans to expand the empire into central Europe. The frontiers held only because of the capable administration of the provincial governors and the settlement arrangements that Aurelius had made with the tribes on the Danube.

The emperor's particular hobby was gladiatorial combat. Commodus loved to watch it and, even more, to take part in it. He would perform in the amphitheater dressed as Hercules, shooting or clubbing to death wild animals. He made the senate officially recognize him as a god as a reward for these achievements. Such behavior earned him many enemies among the upper classes, and his disastrous rule was brought to an end prematurely in 192 CE, when conspirators bribed his regular wrestling partner to strangle him. On Commodus's death, the senate declared him *damnatio memoriae*, meaning that his reign was expunged from official records.

This mosaic depicting a gladiator was found in Torre Nueva, a town in the Roman province of Hispania (present-day Spain).

The empire for sale

The assassins of Commodus put forward the 66-year-old Helvius Pertinax, the prefect of Rome, as a candidate for emperor, and he was accepted by the senate. Pertinax made a good start to his reign when he attempted to restore the financial stability of the state by curbing expenditure. He had no personal wealth, however, and he incurred the wrath of the Praetorian Guard because of his inability to pay them the tribute that was customary on an emperor's accession. They murdered him in 193 CE.

Titus Flavius Sulpicianus, Pertinax's father-in-law and a wealthy senator, then offered the Praetorians 20,000 sesterces each for the throne. His colleague, the aging but even more wealthy Didius Julianus, outbid him, offering each Praetorian 25,000 sesterces. The soldiers accepted the offer and escorted Julianus to the senate, which could do nothing but confirm his nomination. The principate had become a commodity to be bought and sold.

The rise of Severus

When news of the "sale" of the principate reached the provinces, three powerful armies challenged the authority of Julianus, beginning the civil war of 193 CE. The army nearest to Rome was that situated on the Danube River, and it declared its commander, Septimius Severus, emperor in May. Severus entered Rome without opposition. The senate accepted him and, at the same time, condemned Julianus to death.

In Syria, the legate Pescennius Niger had been nominated as emperor by his troops, while in Britain, Clodius Albinus was nominated by his. In an attempt to neutralize part of the opposition, Severus gave Albinus the title of Caesar, which was now used to designate the heir apparent to the throne. This move made Albinus an ally, temporarily, at least. Then, in a brilliant campaign, Severus marched on Niger, dislodging him from his new conquests near the Black Sea and finally defeating and killing him in 194 CE.

Two years later, Albinus proclaimed himself Augustus, a title that implied a share in imperial power. He proceeded to invade Gaul, where he met the army of Severus at Lugdunum (present-day Lyon, France) in 197 CE. In a hard-fought

Pescennius Niger, depicted here in a bust, was nominated as emperor by his Syrian troops. However, he was defeated by his rival Septimius Severus.

battle, Severus proved victorious. Albinus was killed, leaving Severus as the undisputed emperor.

First of the Severi

Severus's reign ushered in the short-lived dynasty of the Severi. The Severan emperors imposed what has been called a military monarchy on the Roman Empire. The emperor dominated both the army and the senate and dictated all new legislation. Severus himself had been born into an aristocratic provincial family in the city of Leptis Magna, near Tripoli in northern Africa, and had held both political offices and military command. In 180 CE, he had married Julia Domna, whose father was ruler of the Syrian city of Emesa and high priest in the temple of Baal (see box, page 140). Julia was to exert great influence on her husband and even rule the empire while he was at war.

Severus sought to exploit the popularity of the Antonine emperors by declaring himself the adopted son of Marcus Aurelius. He also named his eldest son, later to be known as Caracalla, Marcus Aurelius. However, the policies Severus pursued were quite different from those of his popular predecessors. His focus was provincial rather than aristocratic, and he never forgot that he owed his position to the army of the

The Severan Arch was built in the Libyan town of Leptis Magna around 203 CE in honor of the emperor Septimius Severus, who was born in the town.

137

Work on the Baths of Caracalla was begun during the reign of Septimius Severus but finished during the reign of his son, whose name they bear.

Danube. Severus established a new social order dominated by equestrians (members of the mercantile middle class) and opened both military and civilian careers to the lower classes. As for his faithful Danube army, he placed his elite officers in charge of the Praetorian Guard and enrolled three new legions under equestrian command. He also added thousand-soldier auxiliary units to both the infantry and the cavalry.

The Severan revolution extended throughout the administration. Severus reduced the privileges of the peoples of the Italian Peninsula and increased those of easterners and Africans, recruiting the latter to government posts for the first time. Severus had a keen interest in the processes of the law, and he appointed a famous jurist, Papinian, as Praetorian prefect and commissioned him to systemize the law, a move that gave Severus the opportunity to involve his office in the administration of justice.

Severus at war

Severus proved himself an energetic campaigner in foreign affairs. In the east, the Parthians had supported Niger in the civil war, and after defeating his rival claimant, Severus invaded Mesopotamia. However, he was soon called away to deal with Albinus in the west and had to conclude a hasty peace with the Parthians. In the summer of 197 CE, Severus returned to the east to punish the Parthian king, who had attacked the Roman frontier. Severus defeated the Parthians and annexed Mesopotamia as a new province. On his return to Rome, Severus built a triumphal arch in the Forum Romanum to glorify his success against the Parthians.

Severus's other main campaign took place in Britain, where tribes from Scotland had penetrated as far south as Eboracum (present-day York). Although the governor had succeeded in bribing them to return north of Hadrian's Wall, Severus embarked on a punitive expedition in 208 CE. While extensive repairs were carried out to the wall, which had been badly damaged during the Picts' invasion, Severus and his sons conducted raids on the aggressive northerners. Although they failed to bring the invaders to battle, the Roman show of strength seems to have had an effect; there were no more incursions for almost a hundred years. Severus fell ill during this campaign and died at Eburacum in 211 CE.

Caracalla

Severus had intended that his two sons, then in their early twenties, should rule jointly on his death. However, this arrangement did not suit the elder son, Caracalla. Within a year of his father's death, Caracalla had arranged for his younger brother, Geta, to be assassinated. Geta died in the arms of their mother, Julia Domna.

Caracalla considered himself to be a god and believed that his father had ascended to the sun on his death. Caracalla's reign was characterized by extravagance, debauchery, and cruelty. However, he continued the egalitarian social policies and judicial and legislative changes begun by his father. In 212 CE, Caracalla conferred Roman citizenship on all free inhabitants of the empire, so that, for the first time, everyone in the empire had equal status. Because certain taxes were paid only by Romans, this move may have been partially motivated by financial considerations.

Caracalla spent freely. He increased the pay of the ordinary soldiers, in spite of a shrinking treasury, and embarked on an extensive building program, including completing the great public baths begun by his father. These baths became known as the Baths of Caracalla. To help cover the costs of all the projects, Caracalla increased the taxes on senators and doubled inheritance tax and emancipation tax (the tax paid by manumitted or freed slaves). He also debased the coinage by introducing a new silver coin, the antoninianus, which had a face value of

In this undated modern illustration, the emperor Elagabalus leads a dance in celebration of the sun god Baal.

BAAL

Baal was a very ancient fertility god, worshipped by the Canaanites and Phoenicians as early as 3000 BCE. He was originally believed to be a storm god who brought the rain that was essential for growing crops. Many temples were dedicated to Baal. A number of rituals were carried out to placate him, and some of them may have involved human sacrifice.

However, the word *baal* simply meant "lord." Consequently, many other gods in eastern religions came to be called Baal, which explains why the sun god worshipped in Syria in the second century CE was also referred to as Baal.

This sun god, whose name was El-Gabal, was considered to be the lord of the universe. He was often depicted standing beside an eagle, the symbol of divine authority. In Syria, the center of the sun cult was located in the holy city of Emesa, where the emperor Severus's wife, Julia Domna, had been born to the high priest of El-Gabal. When her grand-nephew became emperor, he took the name Elagabalus (son of El-Gabal). He later shocked the Romans with his adherence to the rites of the sun god, reportedly dressing up as the high priest of the god and leading orgiastic processions through the streets of Rome.

two denarii, although it weighed considerably less than one denarius.

Adopting Alexander the Great as his model, Caracalla began an ambitious campaign in the east. However, in 217 CE, while his army was on the march in Mesopotamia, Caracalla was murdered by a group of officers led by the Praetorian prefect Marcus Opellius Macrinus.

Macrinus

Unaware of Macrinus's complicity in the death of their commander, Caracalla's soldiers hailed him as emperor. The senate reluctantly confirmed this appointment. Macrinus was a member of the equestrian order, and was the first *eques* to be made emperor. In his short reign, Macrinus succeeded in completing Caracalla's objective of bringing the whole of Mesopotamia under Roman rule. However, he only managed to do so by paying the Parthians substantial sums of money to give up their claims. In a bid to increase his popularity with the Roman people, Macrinus reduced the military budget and canceled the taxes his predecessor had implemented.

In Syria, a plot was launched to put the grand-nephew of Julia Domna (the late widow of Severus) on the throne. This young man, only 14 years old at the time, was called Bassianus, and he was a chief priest of Baal, the local sun god. The legions in Syria acclaimed him as emperor (having been liberally bribed to do so). The armies of the two rival claimants met in battle near Antioch in 218 CE. The forces of Macrinus were defeated. The emperor himself fled and was later killed.

An exotic ruler

The new emperor, Bassianus, had been brought up in a temple to the Syrian sun god, Baal. He was therefore known as El-a-Gabal, the son of Baal, a name that the Romans changed to Elagabalus. Presented to the senate as the illegitimate son of Caracalla, he also took the name Marcus Aurelius Antoninus.

Elagabalus quickly made himself extremely unpopular with the Roman populace because of his extravagance and outrageous behavior. He appeared in the palace dressed as the high priest of Baal and made it clear that he hoped to impose the worship of Baal on the whole empire. Elagabalus built a temple dedicated to his god in Rome and spent enormous sums of money on religious ceremonies and sacrifices to Baal. Many of Elagabalus's acts seemed sacrilegious to the Romans. For example, when he ordered an ancient statue of the virgin goddess Vesta to be dragged to the temple of Baal, there was a huge outcry

Elagabalus also outraged Rome with his sexual behavior. He engaged in openly homosexual relationships (in particular, one with his charioteer Hierocles), and stories of his orgies spread throughout the city. Animosity toward Elagabalus intensified. After four years, the Romans had had enough. The Praetorian Guard murdered him and threw his body in the Tiber. His cousin, Severus Alexander, was installed in his place.

Severus Alexander

Severus Alexander came to the throne in 222 CE, when he was only 14 years old. He was the son of Julia Mamaea, the niece of Julia Domna. Alexander had a very different character from that of his immediate predecessor. Alexander was serious and docile, and he had a high regard for the office of emperor. He ruled with the help of his mother, and for much of the first decade of his reign, the empire enjoyed a period of internal peace. The *consilium principis* (the emperor's imperial council, on which lawyers and senators sat) was reorganized and regained its former influence, thereby reinforcing the civilian element of government at the expense of the military.

However, the peaceful times did not last. Around 230 CE, trouble broke out in the east, where the Persians (who had overrun and defeated the Parthians)

This relief, found in the Syrian city of Palmyra, depicts an assortment of Syrian deities.

This brooch contains a coin depicting the emperor Philip I, otherwise known as Philip the Arabian.

proclaimed emperor by his troops, and his short reign ushered in half a century of disastrous civil anarchy, during which time no fewer that 26 emperors were appointed.

Although illiterate, Maximinus was an experienced and competent soldier. He was barely recognized as *princeps* in the empire when, almost immediately, he had to crush two rebellions. When Germans attacked the Rhine border, he quickly restored order there with a victory in 235 CE. In the provinces along the Danube River, trouble was fomented by the Goths, a Germanic people from the coast of the Baltic. These tribes dared to challenge the might of the Roman Empire, plundering Greece and pillaging ships in the Black Sea. Here again, Maximinus eventually managed to reassert the supremacy of Rome.

Despite these successes, Maximinus had not endeared himself to the senate. A simple soldier, he had no time for an educated elite and did not care who knew it. In 238 CE, a group of disgruntled landowners in northern Africa joined with the senate in a rebellion against the emperor. The insurgents proclaimed Gordian I, the proconsul of Africa, as the new emperor; he, in turn, nominated his son, Gordian II, as his successor. However, within weeks, both Gordians were dead, killed in a conflict with Capelianus, a Numidian governor loyal to Maximinus. Maximinus then marched on Rome, but he was killed by his own army before he could set foot in the city. The response of the senate was to place Gordian III (the grandson of Gordian I) on the throne.

attacked Mesopotamia in an attempt to win back some of their long-lost territories. Although poorly suited to the role of warrior, the emperor saw it as his duty to go into battle. After a defensive war in the east, the princeps traveled to the Rhine, where there were also threats of invasion. There, in 235 CE, during a riot among the troops in Moguntiacum (present-day Mainz), Alexander was killed. His death brought the Severan dynasty to an end.

Maximinus

The riot in which Alexander was killed had been instigated by Maximinus, an uneducated provincial soldier from Thrace. Maximinus was immediately

The soldier emperors

Only 13 years old when he became emperor, Gordian III held power for five years, during which time the Persians invaded Mesopotamia and Syria, reaching as far as Antioch. On campaign against the Persians, Gordian was murdered in 244 CE by Philip the Arabian, an Arab who had made a career in the Roman army. Philip made peace with the Persians by ceding part of the empire to them and paying a cash tribute. He also secured victories over the German tribes in 246 CE and the Carpi in Dacia the following year. His fabulous victory celebrations in Rome coincided with the city's one thousandth anniversary. The Roman people wanted to believe that a period of peace and prosperity had begun. However, events proved that this was not to be the case.

Another pretender, an officer called Decius, who commanded the troops in Dacia, invaded Italy and fought Philip at a battle near Verona in 249 CE. Philip and his young son were killed, and Decius entered Rome in triumph. As the new *princeps*, Decius attempted to eradicate the eastern religions that had infiltrated the empire, including the imperial residence. These religions included Christianity, and Decius seized all church property and demanded a declaration of loyalty from his subjects, compelling them to make sacrifices to the gods of state in front of official witnesses. Many Christians refused to comply and died for their convictions.

Decius's attack was a heavy blow for the Christian community. Since the time of Marcus Aurelius's rule in the late second century CE, Christians had generally been left in peace. Some had won converts in the highest Roman circles. Now, many of these new believers renounced their faith rather than die as martyrs.

When, in his bid for the principate, Decius left Dacia, the region around it became vulnerable to attack. In 251 CE, a tribe known as the Goths crossed the

This painting by the Flemish artist Peter Paul Rubens (1577–1640 CE) depicts the Roman emperor Decius dying at the Battle of Abrittus.

Danube and invaded Roman territory. Decius hurried back to Dacia to confront them. However, he walked into an ambush. Decius was killed, and his army was totally destroyed.

Father and son

After a series of short-lived emperors, two Roman senators, father and son, began to reign jointly in 253 CE. The father, Valerian, had great personal integrity, but his qualities were not enough to restore the might of Rome. The anarchy of the previous few years had resulted in a crumbling border, and the forces stationed there could no longer repel the onslaughts of the surrounding tribes. While his son Gallienus attempted to hold the line on the Rhine, the Danube, and in Spain, Valerian confronted the Persian king Shapur I in the east. In 258 CE, Valerian was taken prisoner by the Persians. He died in captivity two years later—an unprecedented humiliation for a Roman *princeps*.

Gallienus was left to rule on his own. He faced formidable difficulties and did not have sufficient forces to deal with them. The borders of the empire needed constant defense, and rival kingdoms were set up in Gaul and in Palmyra (see box, page 146). To ensure that his army operated at maximum efficiency, he only appointed *equites* to positions of high military command, a move that antagonized the senate.

Gallienus was an educated man and had a particular interest in Greek culture. He was an adherent to the ancient Greek cult of Demeter. However, he was tolerant of all sects and halted the persecution of Christians. These acts made him extremely unpopular among the traditionalists of the Roman elite.

This rock relief depicts the Persian king Shapur I on horseback. Shapur took the Roman emperor Valerian prisoner.

THE RIVAL STATE OF GAUL

In 259 CE, the legions in Gaul appointed their commander, Marcus Postumus, as *princeps*. Recognized in Gaul, and later in Spain and Britain, Postumus set up in present-day Trier what might be called a "government in exile," complete with a senate and annually elected consuls. He issued his own coins and maintained his own Praetorian Guard. His vast rival empire remained stable for eight years, during which time he defended the Rhine border against incursions by the Germanic tribes. Eventually, Postumus was killed by his own soldiers. He was replaced by Tetricus, the governor of Aquitania. Tetricus was defeated by the emperor Aurelian in 274 CE, bringing the rebel state to an end.

After a number of campaign victories on the Rhine and the Danube, Gallienus found his resources stretched too thin to combat the governments in Gaul and Palmyra. When he returned to Italy to confront one of his generals, Aureolus, who was attempting to usurp the throne, Gallienus was murdered by his own officers in Mediolanum in 268 CE.

The Illyrian emperors

After the assassination of Gallienus, the army appointed an Illyrian, Claudius II, as their emperor. Almost immediately, he had to face a serious invasion by the Goths, who were determined to occupy the Balkan Peninsula. In a brilliant campaign, Claudius inflicted a savage defeat on the invading tribes, putting an end to the Gothic menace for the next 100 years. However, his reign was cut short when he died of the plague in 270 CE.

Claudius was succeeded by several more Illyrian emperors, all of whom tried energetically to restore stability to the empire. The first of them was Aurelian, who ruled from 270 to 275 CE. Aurelian did much to arrest the decline that the empire had experienced in the previous 40 years.

PALMYRA

After around 260 CE, the prosperous desert city of Palmyra in Syria became increasingly powerful under the rule of Odaenathus, the Roman governor appointed by Gallienus to maintain law and order and keep the Persians at bay. The people of Syria organized their own guerrilla bands to assist Odaenathus, who ultimately defeated the Persians near Carrhae.

Odaenathus began to call himself the king of Palmyra. However, he never attempted to take over as emperor, nominally recognizing the authority in Rome. He proved to be a gifted ruler, and Gallienus could do nothing but offer his approval, first with the title Imperator and later with Inspector of all the East.

When Odaenathus was murdered around 268 CE, his widow, Zenobia, immediately took control. She bestowed all of Odaenathus's titles on her infant son, Vaballathus, and set up an independent eastern monarchy in the Persian style. At that time, the emperors in Rome were fully occupied repelling barbarian invasions in Europe, so Zenobia embarked on a campaign to expand her kingdom. In 269 CE, she invaded Egypt, deposed and killed the Roman prefect governing the country, and had herself declared queen. Zenobia then conquered Anatolia, Syria, Palestine, and Lebanon.

Once the Roman emperor Aurelian had successfully dealt with his rivals in Europe, he turned his attentions to the east. Aurelian recovered Rome's former provinces with relative ease and defeated Zenobia in battle at Immae and Emesa. She was later captured and taken to Rome as a captive. Aurelian showed mercy on the former queen and spared her life. Zenobia later married a Roman senator.

This relief from Palmyra depicts Queen Zenobia, who helped to establish the Palmyrene Empire in the late third century CE.

Aurelian had been a cavalry officer in the army of Gallienus, and his reign was marked by a number of important military successes. He successfully drove the Vandals from Pannonia and the Juthungi from the Danube region. Aurelian then had to defend northern Italy itself. A tribe called the Alemanni crossed the Po River, but Aurelian defeated them decisively. Because their attack had threatened Rome itself, Aurelian began the construction of a great protective wall around the city in 271 CE.

Aurelian pragmatically abandoned Dacia as being too difficult to defend. However, in the east, he was more aggressive. In 272 CE, he embarked on a campaign to recapture the lands lost to Queen Zenobia of Palmyra. He was immediately successful, as city after city surrendered to his forces. Aurelian then went on to Gaul, where he restored Roman rule in 274 CE.

On the domestic front, the economy was threatened with collapse, the result of Gallienus issuing virtually worthless coins. Aurelian called in much of the debased coinage and issued new coinage, reintroducing the antoninianus. This move did not altogether stem inflation, so to pacify the populace, he instituted a daily issue of bread, plus regular distributions of salt, oil, and pork.

Aurelian was outstandingly successful in restoring Roman authority throughout the empire, yet he, too, was eventually murdered by a group of officers. He was followed by a series of six competent generals over a nine-year period; all of them continued to purge the empire of invaders and revolutionaries.

The Aurelian Wall was built to protect Rome from barbarian invasion. It was completed in 275 CE.

See also:

The Disintegration of the Empire (page 148) •
The Edges of the Empire (page 126) •
Expanding the Empire (page 100)

THE DISINTEGRATION OF THE EMPIRE

In the third and fourth centuries CE, the Roman Empire was rarely united or stable. For much of the period, rival claimants fought each other for the throne. At the same time, the Germanic tribes of northern Europe constantly threatened the empire.

The third century CE saw the Roman Empire in crisis. Its economy was in ruins, its social order was disintegrating, and its army was too small to either police the enormous empire or protect its borders from foreign aggression.

The problems with the army were manifold. It was not only too small, but also too static. Garrisons set up to protect the provinces or the frontiers rapidly became permanent towns, and many new recruits came from the local area. Far from Rome, the soldiers felt they owed allegiance only to their own legion and general, rather than to the emperor. Some units of the army consisted of tribal mercenaries, sometimes under their own chieftain. Such units were not amenable to traditional army discipline and resisted the rigorous training that characterized the army of old. Insubordination was rife, leading to frequent revolts and occasionally assassination of the commanders.

The army was also expensive to maintain. Military pay had been increased under Caracalla, and troop bonuses were often paid following a successful campaign. To augment the soldiers' pay, some generals allowed the legionnaires to plunder—even in the provinces. During the third century CE, the general population was victimized as frequently by Roman soldiers as by invading barbarians.

The state of the economy

As the empire grew ever more expensive to administer, successive emperors attempted to address the problem by debasing the coinage. They gradually decreased the proportion of gold, silver, and copper in the coins, which resulted in a decrease in their actual value. Prices soared, and rampant inflation brought poverty and misery to many of the citizens. In addition, the emperors levied the highest taxes in history.

The economic crisis hit trade hard. Artisans were unable to sell their products, and people had no money to buy imported goods. Increasingly, the provinces had to rely on their own resources. As the coinage became ever more worthless, barter became popular, and many taxes were paid in kind. This development made things difficult for tax collectors, who were personally responsible for delivering the correct amount of tax to the government. Many collectors tried to evade their commitment by disappearing into rural isolation.

Epidemics also contributed to the empire's general decline. Outbreaks of disease regularly wreaked havoc on the

This relief showing Roman legionnaires at work dates to the reign of Trajan in the early second century CE, when the empire was at the height of its power.

population, decimating it and reducing the supply of labor needed to work the land and repair roads and aqueducts. The number of slaves also declined, because the army no longer engaged in profitable wars that brought tens of thousands of prisoners to the slave markets.

To make the most from their land, landowners turned to different ways of farming. Instead of using slaves to work an entire estate, owners leased parcels of land to farming families. These tenant farmers agreed to surrender a fixed share of all their income to the landowners. This arrangement, while it provided lower profits than before, did at least guarantee the landowners a regular income, which was important at a time when it was difficult to find a market for wine, oil, and other estate products.

The arrangement was also beneficial to the tenant farmers (or *coloni*, as they were called), providing some measure of protection in unsettled times. Occasionally, a small landowning farmer would even offer his acreage to a wealthy landowner in return for a contract as a tenant farmer. As the system became increasingly widespread, landowners attempted to tie their *coloni* to the land. In the fourth century CE, the emperors would force successive generations of *coloni* to stay on the estates, making them little better than serfs.

The last Illyrian emperors

After Emperor Aurelian died in 275 CE, the senate appointed an elderly senator called Tacitus to be his successor. Tacitus resigned (or was killed) in less than a year and was followed by the Illyrian general Probus. Probus successfully fought off a Gallic invasion and then turned his attention to economic reform. He employed the army on various public

works programs, brought in barbarians to settle the provinces, and encouraged the cultivation of abandoned farms. These measures did not make him popular with the army, and he was assassinated by soldiers in 282 CE.

The army replaced Probus with Aurelius Carus, a general who shared power with his two sons, Numerian and Carinus. Carus and Numerian were both assassinated two years later while on campaign in Persia.

After the death of Numerian in 284 CE, yet another Illyrian, called Diocles, seized power. The son of a farmer, he had risen through the ranks to become a popular general in the army of Carus. When Numerian was murdered by Aper (his father-in-law), Diocles promptly killed Aper and was himself proclaimed

The emperor Aurelian, depicted on this coin, helped temporarily halt the decline of the Roman Empire.

emperor by the troops. Changing his name to Diocletian, the new emperor subsequently defeated and killed Carinus.

Diocletian's hold on power was precarious. Persians threatened the empire in the east, while Germanic tribes harassed the north. The loyalty of Gaul was in question because of the *bacaudae* (armies of escaped *coloni* reneging on their obligations) and displaced farmers ruined by war and exploitation. To reestablish Roman authority in these areas, Diocletian needed to send in experienced commanders. However, he was aware that, in the past, victorious generals had often seized power, as he himself had done. In order to bypass this problem, he decided to share power with his generals.

The tetrarchy

Diocletian established a new form of government, a four-way sharing of imperial power called the tetrarchy. He first invited the general Maximian to share power, giving Maximian the titles Caesar (in 285 CE) and Augustus (in 286 CE). Then, in 293 CE, Diocletian selected two more generals and gave them each the title Caesar. He adopted one of them, Galerius, as his son, while Maximian adopted the other, Constantius. These generals were all Illyrians and were related to Diocletian either by marriage or adoption.

Each "emperor" was given a section of the empire to control, although no formal territorial division was made. Diocletian took the eastern part of the empire, consisting of Thrace, Egypt, and Asia, while Maximian had the Italian

This marble head, created in 299 CE, depicts Diocletian, who succeeded in stabilizing the empire.

Peninsula and Africa. Galerius ruled the Danubian provinces, while the western provinces of Gaul, Spain, and Britain went to Constantius. Each emperor had his own capital city in his region; none of them resided in Rome. Diocletian retained overall supervision of the empire and the authority to legislate and appoint consuls.

The system effectively restored stability to the threatened areas and improved provincial government. Provincial armies were increased in size, particularly in the border areas, and landowners were

The four members of Diocletian's tetrarchy are depicted in this fourth-century-CE sculpture.

required to contribute either money or recruits to the army. Diocletian also established a tactical army under his direct control. The tetrarchy effectively ended the supremacy of Rome and the Italian Peninsula and, by establishing separate centers of power in the eastern and western parts of the empire, paved the way for its eventual division.

On the domestic front, Diocletian instituted price controls on food and other necessities and established maximum wages for workers. These measures went some way toward curbing the raging inflation. He improved administrative efficiency in the provinces by appointing *equites* rather than senators as the administrators. These appointees were responsible for all aspects of civilian administration, including police and legal matters and, above all, taxation.

The changes that were implemented by Diocletian resulted in enormous increases in the costs of running the state, and these costs had to be met by the populace via increased taxes. To ensure that the taxes were paid, Diocletian organized the empire as a coercive state, enforcing universal cooperation in its maintenance. To preserve the status quo, he insisted that anyone practicing an important profession was compelled to continue it for life and that a son was to follow in his father's footsteps. The *coloni*, the tenant farmers who previously had some right to mobility, were henceforth tied to the land. These measures may have gone some way toward stabilizing society, but they came with a price. For many Roman citizens, freedom was now severely limited.

Diocletian was an autocrat, and he believed that he received his authority from the gods, with whom he would take his place after his death. However, Diocletian also wanted to be considered a god while he was still living, and he invoked Roman religious tradition to support the idea.

THE SPREAD OF CHRISTIANITY

By the second century CE, Christianity was spreading throughout the eastern part of the Roman Empire, and Christian communities known as *ecclesia* (assemblies) were well established in Greece. Initially, the members of these communities were united only by their common faith, and there was no central authority either within the individual groups or over the church as a whole. In time, however, the administration of a community fell to one of its elders, who came to be called the *episcopus* (supervisor), the Greek word from which the word *bishop* is derived. A hierarchy of priests and lower clergy, variously termed deacons or presbyters, formed under the bishop.

By the third century CE, Christianity had spread to the west, and the bishop of Rome had particular influence. Rome was the city of the apostle Peter, the man Christ had said would be the rock on which he would build his church. Regarded as Peter's heir, each succeeding bishop of Rome was seen as the natural leader of the church and would be approached to arbitrate in any communal disputes.

However, the bishop of Rome had little overall authority. The church was actually a federation of separate communities operating on an individual basis. They cooperated to the extent of giving support in time of need, exchanging literature, and providing lodging for members of other communities. This very lack of a centralized structure appears to have been an advantage during times of persecution, because the church could not be put out of action simply by seizing a few of its leaders.

The church grew steadily throughout the third century CE, and the Christians soon formed one of the largest religious groups in the empire. Solidarity, based on their faith, mutual support, and respect for their leaders, was their strength. Although they were often persecuted, they could escape death if they renounced their faith at the last moment. Perhaps many did so, but those who remained steadfast and died were honored as martyrs by the community, and it was believed that their souls went straight to heaven.

In the later part of the third century CE, the empire entered a period of prolonged crisis, when rival claimants fought for the imperial crown and inflation threatened to destroy the economy. Yet it was precisely in these disturbed times that the church gained even more converts. It seems that the promise of a better life in the hereafter and an eternal reward for the righteous appealed to many people.

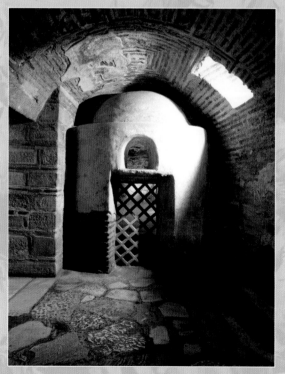

This vault was used for Christian worship in the early fifth century CE. By that point, the Christian faith had spread throughout much of the Roman Empire.

153

This 16th-century-CE painting depicts the flagellation of the martyr Saint Sebastian, who was killed during the reign of Diocletian.

Linking himself with Jupiter, Diocletian demanded to be known as Jovius and to be regarded as a holy person. This move put him in conflict with the Christians, who refused to take part in emperor worship. Incensed by the attitude of the Christians and alarmed by the increasing number of them in the army and in his court, Diocletian became determined to put an end to Christianity once and for all.

The final, and fiercest, persecutions of Christians began in 303 CE, primarily in the east, where Diocletian himself reigned alongside Galerius. Diocletian ordered the destruction of churches and banned Christians from assembling to worship. Many Christians were killed, but regardless of how many martyrs died, the new faith was too firmly established to be extinguished. By the time Diocletian abdicated in 305 CE, the ferocity of the persecutions had diminished.

The succession

After Diocletian had reigned for 20 years, he abdicated and forced Maximian to do the same. The two Caesars, Galerius and Constantius, became Augusti, and two new Caesars, Severus and Maximinus Daia, were appointed. Together, the four made up the second tetrarchy. In this way, Diocletian attempted to replace the hereditary principle with a system of appointing successors. Within a year, however, the system had broken down. When Constantius died in 306 CE at Eboracum (present-day York) in Britain, the armies of Gaul and Britain ignored the rules of the tetrarchy and proclaimed his son Constantine as Augustus. When he heard the news,

Maximian's son Maxentius promptly had himself declared Augustus in Rome, ignoring both Galerius and Severus. Thus, in 307 CE, seven men were claiming to be Augustus (including another pretender in Africa). Civil war followed, but by 311 CE, several of the claimants had died by natural causes or been assassinated, leaving Constantine and Maxentius in the west and Licinius (who had been declared Augustus by Galerius) and Maximus Daia in the east.

Constantine, who was militarily the strongest among them, invaded Italy and defeated Maxentius near Rome in 312 CE. Maxentius drowned while trying to escape. During the campaign, Constantine claimed to have had a vision of the cross, and he later converted to Christianity. After his defeat of Maxentius, Constantine joined forces with Licinius. In 313 CE, they won over the Christians in the east by issuing the Edict of Milan, which guaranteed the Christians freedom of worship. Maximinus Daia was defeated by Licinius and died the same year.

Diocletian, depicted on this coin, is perhaps most famous for his persecution of Christians.

This gold coin depicts the emperor Constantine, who reunited the empire in 324 CE.

Constantine emerged from the contest as the victor in the west, while Licinius ruled in the east. For a time, there was an uneasy truce between the two emperors, but in 324 CE, the tensions between them erupted into war. Licinius was forced to surrender, and he and his son were both executed.

Constantine

Now the uncontested ruler of the Roman Empire, Constantine established a new administrative headquarters on the site of Byzantium and called it Constantinople. Situated on the Bosporus, a strait that links the Black Sea to the Mediterranean Sea, this small town occupied a strategic position between the Euphrates and Danube rivers and between the continents of Europe and Asia. It was therefore an important post on the overland trading routes between east and west, and it was destined to become a major city (present-day Istanbul).

Constantine, who had converted to Christianity sometime around 312 CE, now declared it to be the official religion of the Roman state. The traditional worship of the pagan gods was discouraged; their temples were ransacked and their treasure, together with that of Licinius, was used to benefit the state. To stabilize the currency, Constantine had a new gold coin minted, the solidus, which was to become the basic currency of the Byzantine Empire.

Constantine continued many of the reforms initiated by Diocletian, particularly that of separating civilian power from military power. He maintained the separate forces of border guards (*limitanei*) and tactical troops (*comitatenses*), and he expanded the authority of the Praetorian prefects, establishing four great prefectures: the east, the Italian Peninsula, Gaul, and Illyricum.

Constantine's government was expensive. Among other measures, he organized a distribution of grain to the poor, which made him popular with that segment of the population but not with the taxpayers who had to fund the scheme. The burden fell most heavily on poor farmers and landholders and resulted in widespread anger among taxpayers and corruption among tax collectors.

Constantine's sons

Constantine's death in 337 CE was followed by civil war, as his three sons battled for power. Eventually, in 353 CE, the only surviving son united the empire under his rule as Constantius II. During the eight years of his reign, the eastern border was under almost constant attack by the Persians, while on the Rhine and the Danube, marauding tribes made frequent raids. Constantius himself was only a mediocre general. However, his nephew Julian, whom he appointed Caesar and commander of the Roman army in Gaul, soon proved to be a brilliant military leader. Julian campaigned so successfully in Gaul that his troops

Work on the fourth-century-CE Basilica of Maxentius and Constantine began during the reign of the former emperor and was finished during the reign of the latter.

declared him emperor in 361 CE. Civil war was averted when Constantius died in November of that year.

Julian and Jovian

Although he reigned for less than two years, Julian proved to be an extremely capable administrator. He took steps to curb the extravagance of his court, reduced the power of the secret police, and introduced a stable copper coinage. He renounced Christianity (earning himself the title Julian the Apostate) and reinstated the pagan religion, hoping to restore the traditional values of ancient Rome. Julian was killed fighting against the forces of the Persian Sassanid Empire in Mesopotamia in June of 363 CE.

Julian was replaced by Jovian, who was put in place by the army and lasted for only eight months. A moderate Christian, he attempted to restore religious tolerance to the empire. He succeeded in negotiating a peace with the Persian king Shapur II by ceding a considerable amount of territory, including the city of Nisibis and the whole of Armenia. Jovian died as the result of an accident in February of 364 CE. With his death, the empire was once again divided into east and west.

Valentinian and Valens

Valentinian I, a capable officer and another moderate Christian, was chosen by the army to be emperor in the west.

The ruins of this temple stand in present-day Algeria. Northern Africa was part of the Roman Empire from the second century BCE until the early fifth century CE, when it fell to the Vandals.

157

4-year-old brother Valentinian II. Gratian was a devout Christian and attempted to erase all traces of the ancient Roman religion from the empire.

In the east, Valens was less successful in defending his borders, which were continually raided by barbarian tribes, including the Visigoths from Dacia. The Visigoths, being harassed by the Huns, were driven south over the border and into Roman territory in 375 CE. Valens welcomed them, thinking that they could colonize depopulated land and supply recruits for his army. However, Roman officials began to mistreat the new arrivals, and in 376 CE, the Visigoths rebelled. Valens was forced to go to war.

The next two years saw a number of inconclusive battles. Finally, in 378 CE, Valens confronted an army of Gothic warriors outside Adrianople in Thrace. Earlier in the year, Gratian had driven back the Alemanni and the Goths from the border on the Danube. Valens had been advised to wait for the armies of his fellow emperor to join him before he confronted the Goths. He ignored the advice. In the ensuing battle, the Gothic cavalry inflicted a humbling defeat on the Roman forces. Valens himself died in combat. The Battle of Adrianople was a major turning point in the history of the Roman Empire; the Goths now had control of the Balkan Peninsula.

Gratian and Theodosius

After Valens's death, Gratian declared Theodosius emperor in the east in 379 CE. Theodosius was the son of Valentinian I's famous general Theodosius the Elder, who had been executed in a purge of Valentinian's supporters. Following in

The army insisted that he share power, so he appointed his less capable brother Valens as co-regent in the east. Valentinian proved to be an energetic defender of the empire. With the help of his general Theodosius the Elder, he fought a number of successful border campaigns in Gaul and Pannonia and put down insurrections in Britain and Africa. On the domestic front, he took steps to protect the poor, to maintain a strong administrative and tax collection system, and to encourage religious tolerance. Valentinian died suddenly in 375 CE in a freak manner; he burst a blood vessel in his brain while shouting at an ambassador from the Quadi tribe.

After the death of Valentinian, his 16-year-old son Gratian became emperor in the west, sharing his rule with his

This coin bears the profile of Magnus Maximus. The commander of Roman forces in Gaul and Britain, Maximus was proclaimed emperor in 383 CE.

his father's footsteps, Theodosius was also an outstanding army general and was destined to emerge victorious from a very turbulent time. In 382 CE, he made peace with the Goths, giving them permission to live within the empire under their own laws and leaders. He did so only on condition that they served in his army.

In 383 CE, Magnus Maximus, the commander of the army in Gaul and Britain, was proclaimed emperor by his troops. He subdued Gaul and killed Gratian at Lyon. At first, Theodosius was disposed to recognize Maximus because they were both Spaniards and orthodox Christians. However, when Maximus invaded Italy, Theodosius met him in battle and killed him in 388 CE.

Valentinian II and Eugenius

Since 375 CE, Gratian had nominally shared the western throne with his brother Valentinian II. Theoretically, Valentinian ruled over Italy, Africa, and part of Illyricum, but because he was only four years old when he became emperor, power in the early years really rested with his mother, Justina. In 387 CE, when Maximus invaded Italy, Valentinian sought refuge with Theodosius, and after Maximus was killed, Theodosius reinstated Valentinian as the emperor of the west. However, Valentinian died in 392 CE, either by assassination or suicide. He was succeeded by Eugenius, who began to reestablish the worship of the old gods of Rome. This policy brought him into conflict with the Christian Theodosius.

Theodosius and Eugenius fought each other at the Battle of Frigidus River

in 394 CE. Theodosius was victorious, making him emperor of both east and west. He was the last man to rule over a unified Roman Empire, but he died only four months later, in January of 395 CE. The empire was then divided between his two sons. The western empire was to collapse in the fifth century CE, while the eastern empire would survive for another thousand years.

This coin, issued in 390 CE, bears the image of Theodosius I, the last emperor to rule over a united Roman Empire.

See also:

Daily Life in Rome (page 116) • The Decline of Rome (page 134) • The Edges of the Empire (page 126) • Expanding the Empire (page 100)

GLOSSARY

aedilis government officials in the Roman republic; equivalent to magistrate. *Aediles* oversaw public order, the market, water, grain supplies, and games. Initially, they were officers at the temple of Diana in the Latin League.

Aeneas mythical hero who escaped the ruins of Troy and settled in Italy. His story is the subject of Virgil's epic poem the *Aeneid*.

Alba Longa city in southern Latium; considered the mother city of Rome; according to legend, freed by Romulus and Remus from a usurper; destroyed around 650 BCE.

Amulius mythical usurper of his older brother, Numitor, as king of Alba Longa; separated his niece, Rea Silvia, from her twin children, Romulus and Remus.

Anatolia another name for Asia Minor (part of modern Turkey).

Apennines range of hills and mountains that forms the spine of the Italian Peninsula.

Aquae Sextiae Roman city in Gaul; modern Aix-en-Provence, France.

Ariminum town on Adriatic coast of Italy; site of modern city of Rimini.

Arretium ancient town in western central Italy; now the city of Arezzo.

Ascanius mythical son of Aeneas; according to legend, the founder of Alba Longa, a city near Rome.

Balearic Islands group of islands in the western Mediterranean Sea. The largest are today known as Mallorca, Minorca, Ibiza, and Formentera.

Brutus, Lucius Junius legendary figure who expelled Tarquin the Proud from Rome and founded a republic.

Campania region of southern Italy between the modern cities of Naples and Salerno.

Cannae town in southeastern Italy; site of the worst defeat in Roman history. Hannibal surrounded a Roman army there and destroyed it in 216 BCE.

Capua major Greek colony in southern Italy; first Greek colony to side with Hannibal in the Second Punic War.

Carthage city in northern Africa on the shores of the Mediterranean Sea; now a suburb of Tunis.

censor office in the Roman republic to which two ex-consuls were elected for five-year terms. They estimated the number of citizens for purposes of categorization, taxation, and military service, and they judged moral behavior.

Ceres Roman goddess of agriculture.

Cimbrians people who invaded southern France and Spain around 111 BCE; defeated by Gaius Marius in 101 BCE.

Cloaca Maxima the first public sewer in Rome; completed in the third century BCE.

consul one of two co-leaders of republican Rome. Each consul served only one year in office at a time.

Dacia area of the Carpathian Mountains and Transylvania, in present north-central and western Romania.

dictator magistrate appointed by the Roman senate; given unlimited authority in matters of state and war for six months.

Epirus ancient kingdom that occupied the coastal region of northwestern Greece and southern Albania.

Etruscans ancient people of central Italy whose civilization emerged around 900 BCE, before the founding of Rome.

fasces symbol of the Roman magistrates' legal authority; ax head projecting from a bundle of wooden sticks tied together with a red strap.

Horatius legendary Roman hero who singlehandedly defended a bridge in Rome against the forces of Lars Porsenna and the entire Etruscan army.

Lar (plural: Lares) Roman family deity; originally were gods of the fields.

Latin League ethnic religious federation of Latin cities on the Italian Peninsula; fought against the Etruscans in the sixth century BCE; abolished in 338 BCE, following rebellion against Roman domination.

Latium region of the Italian Peninsula between the Tiber River and the Apennine Hills; the home of the original Latin people.

lictor attendant who waited on Roman magistrates and carried the ceremonial fasces.

Lupercalia (wolves' feasts) Roman festival named for the wolves' skins worn by the participating priests.

Macedonian Wars four conflicts (214–205 BCE, 200–197 BCE, 171–168 BCE, 149–148 BCE) between the Roman republic and the kingdom of Macedonia.

Mamertines mercenaries from Campania who fought on behalf of Syracuse but then deserted the city-state and seized Messana (modern Messina, Sicily) around 288 BCE; later joined forces with the Carthaginians, thereby precipitating the First Punic War.

mare nostrum literally, "our sea"; Roman name for the Mediterranean Sea.

Mars Roman god of war; father of Romulus and Remus.

Messana modern Messina, Sicily; site of an ancient Greek colony.

Mucius Scaevola legendary Roman hero who is said to have saved the city from an attack by the forces of Lars Porsenna.

Muses in Greek—and later in Roman—mythology, nine sister goddesses (daughters of Zeus) who inspired human artistic creativity: Calliope (epic poetry), Clio (history), Erato (lyric poetry), Euterpe (music), Melpomene (tragedy), Polyhymnia (sacred poetry), Terpsichore (dancing), Thalia (comedy), Urania (astronomy).

Numantia Celtiberian stronghold until 133 BCE, when it fell to the forces of the Roman general Scipio Aemilianus; near modern town of Soria, Spain.

Numidia region of northern Africa; roughly equivalent to the area of modern Algeria.

Numitor legendary king of Alba Longa; grandfather of Romulus and Remus; deposed by his younger brother, Amulius.

optimates conservative senatorial aristocracy during the later Roman republic (c. 133–27 BCE).

Ostia ancient town at the mouth of the Tiber River; port of Rome.

Parthians Persian horsemen who gained their independence from the Seleucids around 240 BCE and settled in northern Persia; conquered extensive territory east of the Seleucid Empire; later fought the Romans.

patrician in Rome, an aristocrat; often a member of the ruling class.

phalanx battle array used by the ancient Greeks and Macedonians, consisting of a number of rows of heavily armed infantry soldiers. Thebans later introduced the diagonal phalanx, which had more rows on one side.

Phoenicia area of the eastern Mediterranean roughly corresponding to modern Lebanon.

plebeian any citizen of Rome who was not a patrician (aristocrat); member of the lower classes.

populares patrician political group in the late Roman republic that drew support from the masses against the ruling oligarchy.

Porsenna, Lars legendary sixth-century-BCE Etruscan king who besieged Rome in an unsuccessful attempt to restore a monarchy in the city.

praetors political leaders of the Roman republic; later became known as consuls.

Punic War, First (264–241 BCE) war between Rome and Carthage for supremacy in the western Mediterranean. Rome adopted seafaring armies to defeat the Carthaginian power at sea. By

introducing grappling, they defeated the Carthaginians. Carthage then ceded Sicily to Rome.

Punic War, Second (218–201 BCE) war between Rome and Carthage (under Hannibal) for supremacy in the western Mediterranean.

Punic War, Third (149–146 BCE) war between Rome and Carthage for supremacy in the Mediterranean. The Romans destroyed Carthage in 146 BCE.

quaestor Roman official who originally assisted consuls in criminal justice; eventually, financial manager. The office was often the starting point of a political career.

Rea Silvia legendary daughter of Numitor, king of Alba Longa; became a Vestal Virgin; mother of Romulus and Remus.

res publica **(public things)** republic; Roman state (c. 510–27 BCE) governed by two annually elected consuls. Citizens exercised influence through popular assemblies and the senate.

Rhodes largest of the Dodecanese, a group of islands in the Aegean Sea off the eastern coast of mainland Greece.

Romulus and Remus legendary twin sons of the war god Mars. Separated at birth from their mother, Rea Silvia, they were suckled in infancy by a she-wolf. They later co-founded the city of Rome. Romulus then killed Remus and became the first king of Rome.

Rubicon small stream separating Gaul from the central Roman republic. When Julius Caesar crossed it in 49 BCE—in defiance of a law that forbade provincial generals from leaving the territories to which they were assigned—he precipitated a three-year civil war.

Sabines ancient people who lived in mountains to the east of the Tiber River. According to legend, their women were carried off by the men of Rome.

Seleucid Empire empire that, between 312 and 64 BCE, extended from Thrace on the edge of the Black Sea to the western border of India. It was formed by Seleucus I Nicator from the remnants of Alexander the Great's realm.

senate college of magistrates; the highest authority in the Roman republic.

SPQR initials, written on the standards of Roman legions, representing a Latin phrase that means "for the senate and people of Rome."

Stoicism school of philosophy founded by Zeno of Citium in Athens in the third century BCE. At its core was the belief that people should do what is required of them by nature and accept their lot.

Syracuse Corinthian colony on Sicily; flourished culturally and commercially in the fifth century BCE and dominated the other Sicilian colonies. Syracuse resisted Athenian siege and defeated Athens with the help of Sparta (414–413 BCE).

talent unit of weight and money used by Hebrews, Egyptians, Greeks, and Romans. Its exact value varied from place to place; in Attica, one talent weighed around 57 pounds (25.8 kg).

Tiber second longest river in Italy after the Po.

Titus Tatius legendary king of the Sabines who combined his realm with Rome and ruled with Romulus.

tribune in the ancient Roman republic, a political representative of the plebeians.

tribus **(district)** division where Roman citizens were registered on the basis of landholdings and assessed taxes called *tributum*.

Troy ancient city of northwestern Anatolia (part of modern Turkey); reputed destruction by Greek forces formed the basis of Homer's epic poem the *Iliad*.

Vestal Virgins six priestesses who inhabited the temple of the goddess Vesta.

MAJOR HISTORICAL FIGURES

Agrippa (c. 63–12 BCE) deputy of the Roman emperor Augustus; defeated Mark Antony at the Battle of Actium in 31 BCE.

Antony, Mark (83–30 BCE) Roman general under Julius Caesar and later triumvir (43–30 BCE); became lover of Cleopatra, queen of Egypt, and was defeated with her by Octavian (the future emperor Augustus) in the last of the civil wars that destroyed the Roman republic.

Archimedes (c. 287–212 BCE) Greek mathematician and inventor killed during the sacking of Syracuse by the Romans.

Augustus (63 BCE–14 CE) originally named Octavian; first emperor of Rome; ruled from 27 BCE until his death.

Caesar, Julius (100–44 BCE) Roman general who conquered Gaul (58–50 BCE) and triumphed in the civil war of 49–45 BCE; dictator of Rome (46–44 BCE); assassinated by political opponents.

Caligula Roman emperor from 37 to 41 CE; succeeded by Claudius I.

Cassius, Gaius one of the assassins of Julius Caesar in 44 BCE.

Catiline (c. 108–62 BCE) Roman aristocrat who tried unsuccessfully to overthrow the republic in 63 BCE.

Cato the Elder (234–149 BCE) leading Roman politician who led the republic into war against Carthage.

Cicero, Marcus Tullius (106–43 BCE) Roman statesman and author. On the death of Julius Caesar, he took the side of Brutus.

Cleopatra queen of Egypt from 51 to 30 BCE; ruled successively with her two brothers, Ptolemy XIII (51–47 BCE) and Ptolemy XIV (47–44 BCE), and then with her son Ptolemy XV (44–30 BCE). A mistress of both Julius Caesar and Mark Antony, she and the latter committed suicide together after their defeat by Octavian (the future Roman emperor Augustus).

Crassus, Marcus Licinius (c. 115–53 BCE) Roman politician who formed the first triumvirate with Julius Caesar and Pompey. After Crassus's death, the other two members became enemies and precipitated a civil war (49–45 BCE).

Fabius Maximus Verrucosus, Quintus (died 203 BCE) Roman commander whose delaying tactics during the Second Punic War bought time for Rome to prepare to confront the Carthaginian army of Hannibal.

Hadrian Roman emperor who ruled from 117 to 138 CE, succeeding his uncle, Trajan. His rule was a period of consolidation of the vast empire.

Hamilcar Barca (c. 270–228 BCE) Carthaginian general who made peace with the Romans at the end of the First Punic War; father of Hannibal.

Hannibal (247–183 BCE) Carthaginian general who famously led an army with elephants over the Alps from Spain to Rome.

Jugurtha king of Numidia from 118 to 105 BCE; fought against Rome for control of his realm in northern Africa.

Mithridates king of Pontus (in northern Anatolia) from 120 to 63 BCE; led an uprising against Rome in Anatolia and Greece in 88 BCE; defeated by Sulla in 84 BCE.

Nero Roman emperor from 54 to 68 CE; committed suicide. His rule is best known for its immorality and violence.

Ovid (43 BCE–17 CE) Roman poet; author of *Metamorphoses*; banished from Rome by the emperor Augustus.

Pliny the Younger (c. 61–113 CE) author of nine books of letters on a wide range of contemporary issues.

Plutarch (c. 46–120 CE) Greek biographer who wrote *Parallel Lives*, in which leading Greeks and Romans are discussed in pairs.

Pompey (106–48 BCE) Roman statesman and general; a triumvir (61–54 BCE); first an associate and later an enemy of Julius Caesar.

Spartacus (died 71 BCE) gladiator who deserted from the Roman army and led a slave rebellion (73–71 BCE).

Sulla, Lucius Cornelius (138–78 BCE) Roman dictator who tried to strengthen the republic after its first civil war (88–82 BCE).

Tarquin the Proud traditionally the seventh and last king of Rome; ruled from 534 to 510 BCE.

Virgil (70–19 BCE) Roman poet; author of the *Aeneid*, an epic of the foundation of Rome by fugitives from the sacking of Troy.

Xanthippus third-century-BCE Spartan mercenary general who fought for Carthage in the First Punic War.

INDEX

Shapur I *144*, 145
Shapur II 157
Sicily *8*, 32–33, 36–38, 41, *41*, *59*, *102*
Silius, Gaius 91
Silk Road 133
slaves 14, 21, 34, 44, 56, 57–58, *60*, 116, 125, 150
social war 53–55
socii 31
Sosigenes 70
Spain 42, 47, 50, *59*, 67, 72, 74, 81, 97, 99, *102*, *128*
Spartacus 56, 57–58, *60*
Stabiae 103
Stoicism 92, 112, 125
Sulla, Lucius Cornelius 44, 51, 54–55, *54*, 56, *59*–60
Sulpicius, Publius 54
Syracuse *8*, 41, *41*
Syria *59*, *59*, 61, 64, 74, *102*, 108, 126, *128*, 129, 130, 131, 140, *141*, 143, 146

T

Tacitus 84, 93, 95, 126
Tacitus, Claudius 148, 150
Tarentum 29–31, 32, 41
Tarquinius Priscus, Lucius 9–10
Tarquin the Proud 6, 10, *15*, 24
taxation 34, 44, 47, 84, 102, 139, 140, 148, 152, 156

tetrarchy 151–152, *152*, 154
Tetricus 145
Teutoburg Forest, Battle of 72, *74*, 82, 126
Teutons 51, 53
Thapsus, Battle of *59*, 66
theater 116, 121, 123, *123*
Theodosius I 148, 158–159, *159*
Theodosius the Elder 158
Thessalonica 64
Thrace *128*
Tiberius 72, 81, 83, 84–87, *86*, 89
Tiber River 9, *16*, 76
Tigellinus 95
Titus 100, 103, 109
trade 34, 131, 133, 148
  Etruscans 13
  shops *48*
Trajan 100, 106–108, *107*, 126, 129
Trajan's Arch *108*
Trajan's Column 108, *109*, *110*
Trasimene, Battle of *8*, 39–40
Trebbia, Battle of 39
tribunes 19
tribute 76
Trojans 6, *9*, *10*
tyrants (kings) 6, 8–10, 12, 14, 15, 26

V

Vaballathus 146
Valens 148, 158

Valentinian I 157–158
Valentinian II 158, 159
Valerian 145
Vandals 147
Varro, Gaius Terentius 40
Varus 82
Vercellae, Battle of 53
Verus, Lucius 111, 112–113
Vespasian 97, 100, 101–103, 105–106, 109
Vestal Virgins 6, 9
Vesuvius 100, 103, 104
veto 19
Villanovan culture *8*, 13, *18*, *25*
Vindex, Julius 97
Virgil 6, 78, 80, 94, 125
Visigoths 158
Vitellius 100–101

W

water supply 90, 150
women 14, 21, 78

X

Xanthippus 35–36

Z

Zama, Battle of *8*, 32, 43
Zenobia 134, 146, *146*, 147
Zeno of Citium 125